Breathe

REST, REFLECT, RESET!

CANDACE WRITES

Published by ELOHAI International Publishing & Media:
P.O. Box 64402
Virginia Beach, VA 23467
elohaipublishing.com

Visit www.candacewrites.com to connect with the author.

ISBN: 978-1-953535-06-1
Printed in the United States of America

ENDORSEMENTS FOR BREATHE

"*Breathe* is amazing. It is a well-balanced blend of religion and therapeutic practices. The linkages with the Bible, through directed scripture review, helps to provide a sense of oneness. The reader can feel the authenticity of the pain and struggle and the joy and peace as one moves forward in the journey. This book will provide comfort to many as they journey through their mental health concerns and rely upon the strength that God has always promised. This journey requires inner strength and the ability to be acutely honest with yourself and your truth."

Janice M. Davis, Ph.D., MSW, LCSW-C
Director of Clinical Education
Howard University School of Social Work

"*Breathe* is a compelling read, offering invaluable insight and solutions to mental health. The transparency shared by Candace is not only a breath of fresh air, but is a clear sign that she is out to save lives. No longer do people, particularly in the Body of Christ, have to suffer silently, many suffering for years, feeling trapped within invisible walls. The days of believing that if you seek help outside of prayer, it puts you outside the will of God or even makes you a doubter of your faith are no more. I believe, as is evident in *Breathe*, that just as God anoints us for our purposes in life, He has also anointed clinicians to remedy the needs of His people. I encourage every reader to dive deep into *Breathe*. Be honest with yourself and God. Seek help, get help, rest, reflect, reset, and live well."

Robert Jennings
Executive Pastor, Ekklesia International

"Gosh, I really love so much about this book. I love that Candace makes everything so relatable. Even though the things we read in the Bible took place a long time ago, if we remember that the people we read about are real people, I think it helps us realize our own power and purpose. It also helps us to understand that not being perfect and "fine" all the time is okay!"

Aryn Wright-Thompson
Actress

"*Breathe* is so powerful because Candace literally bares her darkest moments, sharing actual journal entries. In a world where everyone wants to show themselves through a specific angle or filter, Candace lays out all of her scars. This truly is an act of love and sacrifice. I am so thankful Candace allowed God to use her darkest times to help us all realize light and better days in our own lives."

Andrea Wright-Thompson
Entertainment Manager

"*Breathe* is an invitation to begin a personal healing journey at God's pace. It's a safe place that normalizes the expression of pain and knowing where to place it. Readers will walk away informed on the impact of trauma and how the Lord hears, sees, and acts on our behalf. Candace's personal story, along with Elijah's, is proof that God is indeed Jehovah-Rapha."

Brianna Dance, LMSW

"More than just a must-read. *Breathe* is a 'soul-searching journey of a stream of consciousness.' A spiritual reawakening for physical refueling."

Kelvin Owens, MA
Youth Director, Dixon Grove Baptist Church

"I am moved by the revelation that has deeply changed Candace's life. Her story is the secret life of many of God's children. It is a timely book that is so relevant for such a time as this. I was emotionally connected to Candace's book because of a recent suicide attempt by someone remarkably close to me. I will share this book because the trials and temptations Candace experienced and survived will bless the reader, their family, and friends because suicide affects everyone close to that person who has lost the desire to live."

Catherine E. Reid
Associate Minister, First Calvary Baptist of Church Norfolk, VA

"It's time to rip off those bandages - bandages that are hiding our oozing wounds - wounds that won't heal due to the presence of the sharp and decaying debris of our past trauma! Trauma that was culturally, religiously, or plain ignorantly buried by the voices that are surrounding us. Yet, the pain remains. The bleeding of our soul might be invisible to the natural eye, yet it is more real than anything we can see. Candace finally speaks out about a topic that has been taboo in our society and especially in our churches. Thank you for ripping off the bandages, extracting the debris, and allowing the healing to begin. Our beautiful scars will tell the story of how we have overcome."

Petra Spillman
Positive Leadership Ambassador | Author | Publisher | TEDx Visual Storyteller & Speaker Coach

"*Breathe* is practical, lucid, and a riveting piece of work that opens the reader up to discover and understand the origin of their pain. Candace uses the narrative of Elijah, the servant of God, to reveal how God understands and desires to heal you mentally and emotionally. Lastly, the transparency of Candace will just bring comfort as she connects with you through her narrative. A must-read for those in the body of Christ, because depression and mental illness are real, even in the lives of God's people."

Kevin Martin
Pastor, Living Faith Church

"*Breathe* encompasses all of the elements of the modern-day spiritual read: bible study, self-help, and motivational guide. Yet, it possesses the new age instructions on how to stay sane, grow in God, and develop into a mature human being."

Kantis Simmons
International School Success Speaker and Author of Play your 'A' Game

"*Breathe: Rest, Reflect, Reset* is a must-read for those who desire to participate in their mental health wellness authentically. Candace Writes allows the reader to sojourn along with her as she rehearses her struggles with mental illness. *Breathe* brings Elijah, the historical prophet, into the context of the 21st-century modern-day thought by introducing him as a man who was challenged by mental health issues. It offers the readers choice by choosing to unpack their truths by answering thought evoking journaling prompts included in the book! These prompts gently guide and encourage us to actively participate in our healing work, at our own pace, with no timelines, but a willingness to be vulnerable to the process offered to us by the Holy Spirit. Candace creates space for her co-learners (readers) to companion her on her lived experiences of integrating biblical and clinical healing into her daily lifestyle as a way of maintaining her mental health well-being."

LaShawn Demery
First Lady, Bible Way Church of Washington, DC

"Candace Writes delivers a life-changing and thought altering read. *Breathe: Rest, Reflect, Reset* gives a fresh approach to mental health awareness. Candace's transparency gives the reader an in-depth look at the reality of her experiences. Absolutely liberating! I recommend this book to those who desire a different perspective on maintaining mental health wellness through life-giving biblical and clinical strategies."

Bishop Ronald L. Demery, Jr.
Senior Pastor, Bible Way Church of Washington, DC

Dedication

To every person who could have ended their lives, but didn't and decided to pause; instead, you are more powerful than you think. The fact that you're still here after all you've been through speaks volumes about your character and determination to overcome your struggles. In life, we must take a moment to pause when needed. By taking this moment, you learn how to breathe while giving yourself time to rest, reflect, and reset! Therefore, to every person who has felt unseen. To every person who has felt unheard. To every person who has felt unwanted, I dedicate this book to you, and it's my sincere hope that you give yourself space to pause in order to breathe.

Acknowledgements

First and foremost, I have to give thanks, honor, and praise to my heavenly Father. I thank you for saving me from myself. I thank you for rescuing me when I thought I didn't need to be rescued. I thank you for loving me when I felt unlovable. I thank you for covering, guiding, and restoring me. God, thank you!

To my family. Writing a book has been both beautiful and challenging. It has required an innumerable number of hours studying, reading, and writing to bring this body of work to completion, and I could not have done it alone. I could not have done this without my support system, my family, and my friends. Being a mommy of two boys, Bryson and Braxton, I often had to lean on my family and friends. To my mother, Sharon, and my grandmother, Loretta, especially, thank you both. For the many days and nights you spent with the boys ensuring they were well taken care of in order for me to pull away. I also thank my sister, Whitney. All of you, for believing in my dreams, listening to my ideas, and supporting me in every way during this process, thank you!

To Terressa Brown and Michaela Gross of Ms. T's Helping Hands, LLC, you two are the best young nannies and I am so thankful to God for placing you into our lives. Thank you for coming into my home to provide care for the boys. Your commitment has not gone unnoticed.

A very special thank you to my spiritual family, the Demery's. Thank you for your impartation, unyielding support, and love during one of the most challenging seasons of my life. I appreciate the many conversations, but most importantly, all you have poured into me by way of your time and resources.

To my Uncle Kelvin and Aunt Andrea, thank you both for your time. Thank you for reading my book before its release and for giving me your feedback. Being filled with so much wisdom and brilliance, I am glad I have the both of you to lean on!

To my therapist, Ms. Pearson, I could not thank you enough for all that you've done for me. You have opened up my mind in such a way that has changed the trajectory of my life in a positive and boundless way. Thank you for introducing the story of Elijah to remind me that my condition does not change the love God has for me. You have given me the tools I need to manage my life healthily, and I am breathing more relaxed because of it.

Writing a book, again, is beautiful and challenging. Still, due to God connecting me with ELOHAI International Publishing & Media, the process has been more beautiful than I could imagine. I did not know where to begin, what a book outline entailed, and the amount of work that goes into writing a book to master its fullness and richness. Natasha T. Brown, CEO of ELOHAI International, has helped to make my dreams of becoming an author come to fruition. Thank you for being an ear to listen to my creative and innovative ideas, for allowing me to pick your brain, and for walking me through the process from beginning to end. I thank God for you.

Finally, to my amazing children, Bryson and Braxton: you may not fully understand now why I pulled away quite often, hid away in my bedroom, and had books and papers everywhere throughout our home, but as you get older, I hope you will understand the reason behind it. I also hope you will come to know all that your mommy has endured so that you would not have to. This book signifies what God has done in our lives to break generational curses and give rise to generational healing. I love you both so very much.

Table of Contents

WELCOME

From My Heart to Yours

Hey, you are finally here! I have been praying and looking forward to our time together, and a time it will truly be! I have been praying for your heart, mind, and soul. I wondered how you viewed yourself, life, love, and pain at this divine moment in your life. Though I may not know the intimate details of your trauma history, the persons who have caused your heart to break, or what abandonment, rejection, or identity challenges you may have, the good news is God knows. This book is not in your hands by coincidence. God knew you needed it at this critical time in your life as you're standing at a crossroad. You may be on the brink of a mental breakdown, perhaps suicidal thoughts are running rampant in your mind, or you may be exhausted mentally, emotionally, physically, and spiritually and are wondering if God still cares. I'm here to remind you that He does.

I understand how trauma can impact our psyche to a great extent. I also recognize that the elements of unresolved trauma and unhealed pain can cause you to disconnect socially and at times, spiritually, because you haven't found a safe space to share your truth or are too ashamed to go to God because you believe that your present mental and emotional condition is taboo to Him. Or you may have mastered the art of suppression, which according to Oxford English Dictionary, is "the intentional exclusion from consciousness of a thought or feeling." For this reason, you have shown up in spaces as the "strong friend," however, being strong all the time is not healthy nor is it what God wants you to be right now. He wants you to come away with Him and rest. In 2 Corinthians 12:9 (NLT), it reads, "Each time he said, "My grace is all you need. My power works best in weakness." So now I am glad to boast about my weaknesses, so that the power of Christ can work through me." God works best during your weakness because He wants you to cast all of your burdens, your pain, and your discomfort onto Him. Being the "strong friend," if truth be told, is ultimately exhausting and debilitating—to say the least. I know this to be true because I am the "strong friend" as well.

For these reasons, I wrote this book with you in mind. I know that the common denominator in our journeys is found at the root. Whether the root of your pain is rejection, fear, abandonment, or loneliness—the list of our roots could fill the pages of this book as there are plenty more—the point is, we all have a root we need to dig up. Regardless of whether you have a clinical diagnosis or not, this book is still for you because we've all been met with extreme sadness at some point in our lives and felt alone in our journey. Nonetheless, it's during these times in our lives, when we're overwhelmed with unresolved trauma and unhealed pain, that we need God's love, grace, and mercy to remind us of His hand that's still upon us. God's love for you will always remain the same. What you are currently experiencing has not changed His mind about you nor did it catch Him by surprise. As long as you have a pulse, God has a plan! It may be rough right now, but His plans never fail! He will restore your peace, comfort, and joy! Jeremiah 29:11-13, states, "For I know the plans I have for you," says the Lord. "They are plans for good and not for disaster, to give you a future and a hope. In those days when you pray, I will listen. If you look for me wholeheartedly, you will find me." That seals it right there, but first you must take care of yourself and heal from what you're presently enduring.

This is your time to focus on you because you can't keep pouring into the cups of others while yours is empty. You have to begin to give yourself the same love, care, and attention that you extend to others. I had to learn there is beauty in chaos. At times, God's greatest gift to us is allowing our world to fall apart because it gives Him the ability to put it back together with the greatest level of care and attention to place us where we're destined to be. It may not feel or look like it now, but soon you will look back at this time in your life and be thankful for the crushing pain because it gave rise to your healing. Your breaking point is a divine opportunity for you to experience an amazing breakthrough, and trust me, it will be amazing!

This book will serve as a guide to your healing; standing on the blueprint that God has given us in 1 Kings 19 through the story of Elijah who God raised up in Israel to confront its present day king. Prior to entering into therapy, I was familiar with Elijah from the standpoint of the miraculous works God performed through him, however, I was never aware of Elijah's bout with depression and suicidal ideation, and so, we will go further into his story in the coming chapters. For now, I want to take a moment to explain the layout of the book. For the purpose of the study, I use a number of translations of the Bible for context and understanding, however, I do often use the New Living Translation version, but you may use any version that is best for your reading and understanding. In each chapter we partially focus on Elijah's story while I interlace my own narrative for the basis of practicality. The biblical and practical principles collide as we study the blueprint for healing that God wants us to all experience in times of agony and turmoil.

Throughout every chapter there are songs to meditate on, soul-searching questions, and journaling prompts. The purpose of these exercises is for you to identify your triggers and sore spots. Furthermore, you will be searching through the Word of God to find healing scriptures that speak directly to your pain and there are many listed in the back of the book. You will also write out declarations to speak over your life, and create a healthy recovery plan filled with activities that bring you joy! Lastly, in each chapter is Dr. Gloria Willcox's Feeling Wheel. The concept behind the Feeling Wheel is to assist in describing feelings and emotions through a number of feeling words. Before we move forward, let me introduce some key terms that you'll see throughout this book.

Key Terms

Anxiety - The apprehensive anticipation of future danger or misfortune accompanied by a feeling of worry, distress, and/or somatic symptoms of tension. The focus of anticipated danger may be internal or external.

Anxiousness - Feelings of nervousness or tenseness in reaction to diverse situations; frequent worry about the negative effects of past unpleasant experiences and future negative possibilities; feeling fearful and apprehensive about uncertainty; expecting the worst to happen.

Avoidance - The act of keeping away from stress-related circumstances; a tendency to circumvent cues, activities, and situations that remind the individual of a stressful event experienced.

Defense Mechanism - Mechanisms that mediate the individual's reaction to emotional conflicts and to external stressors (e.g., suppression, denial).

Detachment - Avoidance of socioemotional experiences, including both withdrawal from interpersonal reactions (ranging from casual, daily interactions to friendships and intimate relationships).

Dissociation - is a disconnection between a person's sensory experience, thoughts, sense of self, or personal history.

Insomnia - A subjective complaint of difficulty falling or staying asleep or poor sleep quality.

Major Depressive Disorder - a mood disorder characterized by persistent sadness and other symptoms of a major depressive episode but without accompanying episodes of mania or hypomania or mixed episodes of depressive and manic or hypomanic symptoms. Also called major depression.

Major Depressive Episode - A major depressive episode is a period of two weeks or longer in which a person experiences certain symptoms of major depression: feelings of sadness and hopelessness, fatigue, weight gain or weight loss, changes in sleeping habits, loss of interest in activities, or thoughts of suicide. These symptoms are persistent and cannot be easily changed, even if they are contradictory to a person's circumstances. Depressive episodes recur periodically in people diagnosed with major depression.

Mental Health - a state of mind characterized by emotional well-being, good behavioral adjustment, relative freedom from anxiety and disabling symptoms, and a capacity to establish constructive relationships and cope with the ordinary demands and stresses of life.

Mental Disorder - any condition characterized by cognitive and emotional disturbances, abnormal behaviors, impaired functioning, or any combination of these. Such disorders cannot be accounted for solely by environmental circumstances and may involve physiological, genetic, chemical, social, and other factors.

Panic Attacks - Discrete periods of sudden onset of intense fear or terror, often associated with feelings of impending doom. During these attacks there are symptoms such as shortness of breath or smothering sensations; palpitations, pounding heart, or accelerated heart rate; chest pain or discomfort; choking; and fear of going crazy or losing control.

Post-traumatic Stress Disorder - The exposure to actual or threatened death, serious injury, or sexual violence through directly experiencing the traumatic event, witnessing, in person, the event as it occurred to others, learning that the traumatic event occurred to a close family member or friend, the event must have been violent or accidental, or experiencing repeated or extreme exposure to aversive details of the traumatic event.

Self-Destructive Behavior - actions by an individual that are damaging and not in his or her best interests. The individual may not be aware of the damaging influence of the actions or may on some level wish for the resulting damage. The behavior may be repetitive and resistant to treatment, sometimes leading to suicide attempts.

Self-Medicating - is usually associated with individuals who use drugs or alcohol inappropriately to alleviate emotional problems

Substance Abuse - a pattern of compulsive substance use marked by recurrent significant social, occupational, legal, or interpersonal adverse consequences, such as repeated absences from work or school, arrests, and marital difficulties. *The Diagnostic and Statistical Manual of Mental*

Disorders, Fifth Edition (DSM-5) identifies nine drug classes associated with abuse: alcohol, amphetamines, cannabis, cocaine, hallucinogens, inhalants, opioids, phencyclidines, and sedatives, hypnotics, or anxiolytics.

Suicidal Ideation - Thoughts about self-harm with deliberate consideration or planning of possible techniques of causing one's own death.

Trauma - is an emotional response to a terrible event like an accident, rape or natural disaster. Immediately after the event, shock and denial are typical. Long-term reactions include unpredictable emotions, flashbacks, strained relationships and even physical symptoms like headaches or nausea.

Trigger - a stimulus that elicits a reaction. For example, an event could be a trigger for a memory of a past experience and an accompanying state of emotional arousal.

Now that we're done with all of the formalities, I am eager and already excited about God meeting you during this time and the transformation you're about to experience because healing is already yours; you just have to believe it. It all begins with our thoughts. This is why our minds are attacked in such a powerful way, but our God is more powerful. I love you already.

Blessings,
Candace

Prayer

Before, diving into the book, let's invite the Holy Spirit into our time and space together by praying this prayer:

Holy Spirit, I welcome you here. At this time in my life, my soul is weary, my heart is broken, and my mind is troubled. I know the report of my therapist, my clinician, my sponsor, and my family and friends, but I need you to guide, direct, and lead me through my process of healing. Come into my heart. I give you permission to enter in my brokenness and the crevices of my mind and heart that are hidden to the world. I give you permission to dwell in this dark place until the fragmented pieces of me are mended, until my mind is regulated, and until your light shines brightly again in my life. No longer can I carry this burden alone without your help. It's too heavy. The pain is too great. I need you to breathe life back into me for I'm no longer holding on, but hanging on. I'm exhausted, empty, and my tears won't stop falling. To be honest, it feels as though you're absent most days and do not care about the pain I'm experiencing or the many nights that I toss and turn. I know I'm supposed to walk by faith and not by sight, but I need you to help me believe again—to believe in you and to believe in me. I need you to touch every part of me.

Holy Spirit. I'm desperate for you. I recognize that doing it on my own has not gotten me far. Spirit of the Living God, come to my rescue for I know you respond to the cries of your sons and daughters. I'm crying out to you just as David did in Psalm 31:2, saying, "Turn your ear to listen to me; rescue me quickly. Be my rock of protection, a fortress where I will be safe." I need you. Turn to me. Keep me in the palm of your hands. I want to feel safe again because I feel so alone right now. Holy Spirit, you're welcome into my pain, my trauma, my mess, and my brokenness, you are welcome here. I give myself permission to open up my heart to receive all that you've been waiting to bestow upon me. This is my time to heal. This is my time to hear from you. This is my time to rest. This is my time to reflect. This is my time to reset. Holy Spirit, come in and have your way. In Jesus' name, amen!

INTRODUCTION

Breathe

> "For everything there is a season, a time for every activity under heaven. A time to be born and a time to die. A time to plant and a time to harvest. A time to kill and a time to heal. A time to tear down and a time to build up." - Ecclesiastes 3:1-3

I woke up unusually early this Saturday morning. I looked in the mirror, and the reflection I saw was not the woman I thought I had become. No, who I saw was the hurt, broken, and scared little girl I so desperately tried to help heal throughout the years. I immediately felt like a failure. Painful flashbacks overtook my mind—a little girl, me, hiding in a dark room, terrified. I couldn't breathe. It was as if my present trauma and the trauma from my past collided, transforming itself into hands wrapped around my neck, choking the life out of me. My face stained with dry tears from the night before. Stained wine glasses on the bathroom countertop. My lips chapped, curls all over my head, eyes heavy and swollen from excessively crying, and my shirt hanging off of my shoulder. I could hear the sound of my boys playing in the living room with my now ex-husband. I was still in my pajamas. I grabbed my phone and put on my shoes, and walked out of the bedroom. I greeted everyone, and without giving a reason, I left the house telling them, "I will be back shortly!" As my hand touched the doorknob, I began to cry because I wondered if they would see me again. I opened the door and shut it quickly, walking down the stairs to my car. My cries became uncontrollable, and I was gasping for air. My sobbing then turned into moans and screams as I frantically tried to hold it together as neighbors were walking by, but I couldn't. It was a painful and tearful release that was long overdue for me.

I entered my car, and I drove to the nearest park. I sat there for what seemed like minutes, but I was there for hours, maybe even half the day. In the midst of me sitting in the car, every memory of abuse that I suffered, every person who walked out of my life, every broken promise, every tragic event—it all crossed my mind. Here I am with two boys, on the brink of a divorce, living in a foreign country far away from family and friends, and every bit of the pain I felt in my life all hit me at one time like a ton of bricks. Sitting in my car, Satan began speaking ever so loudly, "No one cares about you. No one understands you. Look at all you've suffered. You're a failure. If you truly want peace and for the pain to stop, you will take your life right now! You don't deserve to live!" Grievously, I believed all the lies Satan told me that day. I texted my now ex-husband apprehensively, waiting in urgency for his response asking, "Do you think you and the boys are better off without me?" After reading his response encouraging me to return home, I sat in the car for a few more hours, drifting in and out of sleep. Crying, hitting the steering wheel and sitting with my loud thoughts. As the minutes continued to pass by, God didn't answer my prayer and plea to die that day because, this moment wasn't my first encounter with suicide, and as you continue to read, you will see it won't be the last. But back to the moment in the car. For that reason, I returned home. This particular encounter with suicidal ideation happened over a year ago. Following this moment, I continued to wrestle with anxiety, depression, and thoughts of suicide for another nine months before I would attempt taking my life for the last time. I had to experience this, I didn't know then, but as I am writing this book I now understand fully why I had to go through all of the pain, the sleepless nights, and agony. God saved me from myself and He did so in such a loving way while showing me the healing blueprint I needed to take back the power over my mind, and now I am sharing it with you.

In 1 Kings 19, God teaches us firsthand how to heal as He restored Elijah to a place of good health emotionally, mentally, physically, and spiritually. God extended grace, compassion, and understanding amid Elijah's agonizing and intense struggle to take his life. Wow! How great is our God? He didn't condemn, rebuke, or shame Elijah, or analyze his faith or lack thereof at the moment—no, He knew what Elijah needed. God had Elijah undergo the three phases of healing that you will continue to learn about as you read and learn more about Elijah's story: a time to rest, reflect, and reset. God gave Elijah time to rest from the agony he was experiencing, a time to reflect and put language to his pain, and then time to reset his mind to continue on the journey ahead. Let me tell you, reading, studying, and learning from Elijah's bout with depression and thoughts of suicide was a moment of self-awakening for me because I no longer felt alone and guilty for the struggle I was facing. I felt seen, heard, and attended to because I knew if God met Elijah's needs, then surely He would meet mine. I pray you believe this as well for yourself.

However, let me caution you, going through the process of healing was not easy for me. It was messy. I spent many nights crying and going before God with my grueling and tormented way of thinking. I understood if I wanted God to heal me then I must stop pretending and suppressing and be real with myself because God can't heal the pretend me, but the real, broken, hurt, and distraught me. In this season of your life, it is not a race to the finish line, it will require you to show up and face your pain head on, but at a safe pace. Therefore, create a tempo to heal as God speaks to you. As you flow through my narrative, as well as Elijah's, this book will cause you to discover the roots that give rise to your tears. The memories that you've shoved down and locked in a dark room are about to open. You're about to give voice to your pain and identify what triggers you in order to better understand your responses to trauma. Has your body responded yet by reading this? Have unpleasant thoughts come to mind? Are you becoming anxious? If you have already had a response to what you've read, it's okay. Remember you are in a safe place. God is in the valley with you and will be with you every step of the way. He was there then, is there now, and is already in your future waiting for your arrival. As you will discover, God showed Elijah grace during his bout with depression and suicidal ideation, therefore, give yourself the same grace. Be kind to yourself and do what you need to do for you because God has already begun a great work within you. S.C. Lourie beautifully wrote, "Let your heart breathe, sweet soul. Breathe deep until you remember life's beauty again. Breathe as much as you need to, until you remember your own beauty again. Take as much time as you need. The world can wait."

With that in mind sis, you deserve a moment to pause, catch your breath and do so unapologetically. Bro, we all need these moments especially after enduring traumatic experiences and unexpected losses. Therefore, this season of your life is a time to rest, reflect, and reset. It's your time to weep and heal. I want you to reflect on your life. I want you to go deep and take the hand of your inner child where the healing needs to begin. Grab your Bible and if you read something triggering, breathe, take a moment, flip to the end of the chapter, and write it down. I want you to write down what you're feeling in the exact moment, and what you read that triggered you. Go to God with your raw and unfiltered pain. He can handle it so don't hold back or come with churchy clichés or jargons. Be your authentic self! Again healing is messy; it's not linear and there is no proper timeline you have to meet. Yield to the voice of God and be sensitive to your healing by adhering to what you hear. Take a deep breath as you read each chapter until we get to the end of our journey together, however your journey will continue because we're forever learning and evolving. As you read, also remember Psalm 46:1, "God is our refuge and strength, always ready to help in times of trouble!" Now turn the page, and let's begin with understanding the character and ministry of Elijah.

CHAPTER ONE

A Time to Understand

"Getting wisdom is the wisest thing you can do! And whatever else you do, develop good judgment." - Proverbs 4:7

Chapter Song: Holy Spirit by Bri Babineaux

In order to understand someone's pain you must first know their story. Therefore, to give proper context to Elijah's bout with depression and suicidal ideation, which we will discuss in further detail in the coming chapters, we have to be wise in our understanding of the events that led to his breaking point. Contextually, there isn't any mention of Elijah, his upbringing, or an explanation as to why God raised him up to be one of today's most commonly mentioned prophets in the Bible, but God,

Notes

more often than not, raises up ordinary people to fulfill extraordinary assignments. Prophets, then and today, are heavily used by God to perform miraculous works. They are God's mouthpieces confronting evil rulers, and giving instruction to the people of God. Elijah was one of God's devoted prophets.

Elijah made his biblical introduction in 1 Kings 17. He showed up in Israel to confront one of its most dishonorable and corrupt kings who had ever taken rulership of Israel. I want you to read the entire book and as you do, pause and take a moment while you are reading to answer the questions below. You will have to cross reference other chapters of 1 Kings for assistance in answering the questions. As you read 1 Kings 17, take note of what's currently taking place in Israel that displeases God, but also understand Elijah's character and his commitment to serve and honor God. Use the margins to make any notes that you deem of importance as you read.

STUDY QUESTIONS

1. Elijah was a ______ from Gilead.
2. Reigning over Israel was King ______ and Queen ______ who worshipped ________ the god of ____________ and _________ the goddess and the mother of Baal. **Hint. See 1 Kings 16:29-34**

Notes

3. God uses Elijah to confront King Ahab because he was worshipping _____ and influencing the Israelites to follow suit. God wanted to establish ______ in Israel.

4. Elijah prayed that there would be no ____ or _____ for the next ____ years and ____ months.

5. Why is no dew or rain significant in Elijah's prayer? **Hint. Baal is a fertility god.** ______________________________

____

6. Why did God send Elijah to retreat outside of Israel? ____________________

____

7. What type of animal provided Elijah food? ______________________________

8. Where did God send Elijah? _________

____

9. The widow at Zarephath did not want to give Elijah _____ because she feared there would not be enough for herself and son.

10. Elijah told the widow that the Lord, the God of Israel, says there will ______ be flour and oil left if she did as Elijah requested.

11. When the son of the widow died, Elijah

Notes

stretched himself out over the child ____ times praying to God.

12. What supernatural moment occurred that caused the widow to believe Elijah was a man of God? ________________

____

After reading 1 Kings 17, what are three things you learned about Elijah that spoke to you about his obedience, faith, and willingness to obey God's commands?

____

____

____

Elijah was an ordinary man, human, just like you and I, and God used him greatly. (see James 5:17) His faith reminds us that the same power that dwells within him also dwells within us, and it also reminds us that God doesn't need anyone's approval to use us. For this reason, remember there is a purpose behind what you're currently going through. God sent Elijah into Israel because King Ahab and Queen Jezebel were evil and immoral and turned the people of Israel away from serving Him to serve the false gods Baal and Asherah. If you recall, these are the very people that God used Moses to set free from Pharaoh and his army in Egypt, but how quickly the Israelites forgot. (see Exodus 13 and 14) King Ahab had a great deal of power and influence over the land. As a result, a massive number of Israelites began to worship Baal and Asherah, abandoning their faith and allegiance to the one and only true living God.

As you also read, I pray that you came to the same conclusion as me pertaining to the character of Elijah. He was courageous for stepping to King Ahab in such a confident and powerful way. He was zealous in his response to God's command and acted with great joy even when entering the unfamiliar territory of Zarephath. Furthermore, Elijah was a faithful servant. He faithfully served God and had complete confidence in Him and exuded humility. Elijah understood that all the great works that were being performed through him, like raising up the widow's son from death, was not by his own power, but by the power of God working within him. God showed Himself mighty in the prayers that He answered for Elijah, the first one being ceasing dew and rain and the second one being the miracle of the widow's son. God working through Elijah in such a mighty way should have revealed to the Israelites that He controls the natural forces: the storms, water, rain, and wind. He controls everything. Unfortunately, they still served false gods and followed King Ahab and Queen Jezebel's command. I am sure their disobedience made Elijah

Notes

Notes

frustrated, but he still stood his ground. Again, Elijah was zealous in his approach to completing the assignment God predestined for him. By God performing supernaturally through him, it ultimately strengthened his faith as it was also preparing him for what was about to take place at Mount Carmel.

JOURNEYING THROUGH 1 KINGS 18

In 1 Kings 17, Elijah retreated from Israel and ended up in Zarephath to be taken care of by a widow unbeknownst to him, due to King Ahab wanting him dead. For three years Elijah was in Zarephath, and during the third year God spoke telling him to return to Israel to confront King Ahab. During this time, Queen Jezebel ordered the death of God's prophets killing them all, as she thought, because there was a man by the name of Obadiah who served King Ahab professionally, but in verse three, it tells us "Obadiah was a devoted follower of the Lord." Due to the killings of God's prophets, he hid 100 prophets by placing them in a cave providing them with food and water, which was calculated and dangerous considering the state and division of Israel, and the fact that he was King Ahab's servant.

As Obadiah was out walking one day, he encountered Elijah who returned to Israel from Zarephath per God's command, and

Obadiah immediately fell face down because he recognized that he was in the presence of one of God's faithful prophets. Quickly, fear came upon Obadiah when Elijah directed him to tell King Ahab that he had returned to Israel because as we've already read, King Ahab wanted Elijah dead, and by Obadiah returning to relay a message with no death report, he could have easily been placed on the king's hit list. Now, I want you to read 1 Kings 18 and from your study write in the spaces below what you have concluded about the character and actions of each person or group of persons.

Obadiah

Elijah

King Ahab

Queen Jezebel

Israelites

Notes

Notes

Elijah did not come to play! He was wholeheartedly about his Father's business. Elijah did not back down from King Ahab when the king projected and deflected, placing the blame of the current condition of Israel onto him. King Ahab was narcissistic and condescending, lacking the ability to take full responsibility for his kingship or the lack thereof. However, what I love about Elijah is that the spirit of the Lord was upon him; and he was fully persuaded and confident in God's ability. In verse nineteen, Elijah tells King Ahab, "Now summon all Israel to meet me at Mount Carmel, along with the 450 prophets of Baal and the 400 prophets of Asherah." One might think 850 to one is unpromising and disadvantageous, but again, Elijah was confident in God's ability to show up and show out in front of the Israelites. This was a massive gathering to say the least as thousands upon thousands showed up to Mount Carmel to witness the challenge of the gods to show who is the true and living God. Upon arriving, Elijah told the Israelites they can't be lukewarm believers. They were either to serve God or serve a false god, but they must choose.

Have you ever been in a lukewarm season? I believe we all have been uncertain and unsure, having one foot in the world and one foot in the Word as we try to discover and learn God.

However, the Israelites were another type of lukewarm people; they went wherever the wind took them.

Notes

It is not out of the realm of possibility that the Israelites were fear stricken. They feared man more than they feared God because their silence in response to Elijah asking them to choose which God they would serve spoke volumes. Elijah, one prophet against 850 prophets, was willing to stand alone. He was poised and totally dependent on God's power and ability. Can you recall a time in your life where you had to stand alone in the face of adversity? No one was standing by your side, no one was around to encourage and cheer you on, but you still stood your ground encouraging yourself because you were confident God would make a way? As a result, God showed up and showed out on your behalf for not recanting or backing down. At times when we're met with an unimaginable situation, we must have trust in God to make the impossible possible, and this is what we're seeing taking place at Mount Carmel.

As you read, the prophets of Baal and Asherah were given a bull to sacrifice and place on the wood, but to not set ablaze, calling upon their god to send fire down from heaven setting the bull on fire. As you read, it didn't happen for them. In the midst of nothing transpiring

Notes

on their behalf, Elijah had jokes. Petty might be Elijah's middle name. He mocked Baal and Asherah, and laughed at the extreme and over-the-top actions they were performing and their means of worshipping their god to set the bull ablaze. I hope you had a good laugh reading this part of 1 Kings 18 because I did.

Again, Elijah was p-e-t-t-y! He says in verse twenty-seven, "You'll have to shout louder," he scoffed, "for surely he is a god! Perhaps he is daydreaming, or is relieving himself. Or maybe he is away on a trip, or is asleep and needs to be wakened!" He was taunting them and I am here for it all. But when Elijah was repairing the altar prepared for the Lord and placing the bull on the altar to be sacrificed, he prayed unto the Lord. What is significant is, unlike the prophets of Baal and Asherah, Elijah's prayer was simple: "O Lord, God of Abraham, Isaac, and Jacob, prove today that you are God in Israel and that I am your servant. Prove that I have done all this at your command. O Lord, answer me! Answer me so these people will know that you, O Lord, are God and that you have brought them back to yourself."

Immediately, the Lord's fire fell and consumed everything including the massive amount of water that Elijah requested to be thrown on the wood to show the Israelites that it was impossible for the wood to burn due to the excessive soaking without God's power. Remember, when God is on your side, He will make the impossible possible. King Ahab had thousands of people behind him worshipping Baal and Asherah, but take note, you can have a number of people behind you and be unsuccessful in your endeavors. If you have God on your side, amazing things can be accomplished in your life beyond what you could ever ask for or think.

Following the great challenge in what the Lord had done on Mount Carmel, the Israelites began worshipping God, calling Him the true and living God. I'm sure King Ahab was enraged at this point as Elijah commanded all the prophets of Baal and Asherah to be killed in the Kishon Valley. Afterwards, Elijah prayed earnestly for the rain to return. After praying seven times, a mighty rain began to fall. Elijah experienced a spiritual victory by ceasing the three-year drought as well as showing the Israelites the truth in exposing Baal and Asherah. But in the midst of triumph, what Elijah didn't see coming was the calamity and devastation that met him in 1 Kings 19. After reading 1 Kings 18, what are three things you learned about God, faith, and the willingness to stand alone during certain seasons of your life?

____

____

Notes

STUDY ANSWERS

1. Tishbite 2. Ahab, Jezebel, Baal, Fertility, Asherah
2. False gods (Baal or Asherah), Order
3. Dew, Rain, 3, 6
4. Direct attack on Baal, a god of fertility who controlled the natural earth that provided rain.
5. King Ahab wanted Elijah dead
6. Ravens
7. Zarephath
8. Food
9. Always
10. 3
11. God used Elijah to raise up her son from his death

CHAPTER TWO

A Time to Grieve

"O Lord, don't rebuke me in your anger or discipline me in your rage. Have compassion on me, Lord, for I am weak. Heal me, Lord, for my bones are in agony. I am sick at heart. How long, O Lord, until you restore me? Return, O Lord, and rescue me. Save me because of your unfailing love. For the dead do not remember you. Who can praise you from the grave? I am worn out from sobbing. All night I flood my bed with weeping, drenching it with my tears. My vision is blurred by grief; my eyes are worn out because of all my enemies." Psalm 6:1-7

Chapter Song: Love The Hurt Away by Donald Lawrence

At the end of Chapter 18, Elijah was on a spiritual high after defeating and slaughtering the prophets of Baal and Asherah. God used him to a great

Notes

extent to show all who witnessed the challenge at Mount Carmel that He is the one and true living God. However, in Chapter 19 where we will spend most of our time, following this great victory, King Ahab tells Queen Jezebel what has just taken place and she was outraged. In verse two she says, "May the gods strike me and even kill me if by this time tomorrow I have not killed you just as you killed them." She wanted Elijah dead. Elijah immediately became fearful and ran away from Israel leaving his servants behind to go into the wilderness of Judah where he stopped under a broom tree. If you are not familiar with a broom tree, it is a tall tree that can extend up to 10 feet which provides a large amount of shade. Sitting under that tree was Elijah. He had just experienced a mountaintop encounter and now he is grieving in the wilderness.

Perhaps, Elijah was anticipating a different outcome after the challenge. Be that as it may, he could have believed that King Ahab and Queen Jezebel would renounce their claim to the throne due to the lawlessness and corruption they brought to Israel. However, that did not happen. Queen Jezebel still wanted him dead and Elijah ran. It is not out of the realm of possibility to consider why Elijah ran. Recall all of the miraculous works God performed through Elijah, he knew the

Notes

power that God possesses, and has experienced personal encounters with God, but he ran. Instead of praying to God for his safety or being still until God gave him instructions, he ran. For these reasons, one may allude that running is Elijah's trauma response. It can also be considered that when the spirit of fear was upon Elijah, he responded irrationally which leads me to believe that running was the norm for Elijah and there could be events in his upbringing that when fear was present, running was his means of escaping what triggered him. Running was escaping from the physical threat, but the real threat was in Elijah's mind. His thoughts were tormenting him. Webster defines being tormented as "experiencing extreme pain or anguish of body or mind," and this is what Elijah is experiencing.

Can you recall a time in your life where you ran and tried to escape? You wanted to escape physically by removing yourself from a situation or mentally because your thoughts were too overwhelming. You may have not run out of the state as Elijah ran out of Israel, but are you familiar with running from the place or people that have triggered you? Maybe it reminded you of a traumatic experience or painful time in your life. Or possibly, you have detached yourself from others, stopped showing up to events, entered into an

Notes

isolated state, and stopped answering calls. Everything seemed to be flowing smoothly in your life, and then out of nowhere, tragedy hits, your life is in danger, or you experience a significant loss, and it has caught you completely off guard. Your first response is not prayer, but it's to run because grief has distorted your thoughts and perception of reality. Take a moment and reflect on this time in your life. How did you cope? What did your grieving process entail?

Generally, grief is defined as a loss of a loved one or bereavement. While this is true, Webster also defines grief as "an unfortunate outcome." You may have been expecting your marriage to last, but now you're standing in front of a judge preparing for a divorce—an unfortunate outcome. You've been on countless interviews believing that one of the employers would call you with a job offer, and no one calls—an unfortunate outcome. You were happy and settled into your home, and then tragedy occurred due to a natural disaster, and now you're staying at a hotel wondering what to do next—an unfortunate outcome. Grief

Notes

shows up differently for all of us, but we've all experienced grieving seasons. We all have experienced an unfortunate outcome. Here Elijah sat in the wilderness, weeping, grieving, and feeling like after all he had done, all the miraculous works he had accomplished for God was not enough.

Elijah was distraught, depressed, and experiencing suicidal ideation. He began to pray that he might die and grievously speaks, according to the Christian Standard Bible, saying, "I have had enough! Lord, take my life, for I'm no better than my fathers." Wow! I have had enough. Have you ever reached the point where you believed your life was no longer worth fighting for? Perhaps traumatic experiences have not pushed you to the point where suicide has crossed your mind, but you've had your share of "enough moments!" You're tired—tired of being hurt, betrayed, giving your all to others and not receiving anything but heartache and pain in return. Reflecting back on the moment in the car when I wanted to die, as Elijah endured the same agonizing and tormenting thoughts towards life, was the moment where I began to have enough, I was done, but I have to remember all that led me to that point. Let's go down memory lane for a minute to one of my journal entries.

JOURNAL ENTRY - DECEMBER 2019

Notes

God, I'm in danger. I need you to get me out of this 'self-digged' grave. I need you to get me out of here again. I'm scared here. Lonely here. Distraught and troubled here. I want to live, but God the thoughts that torment me throughout the day and night are taking over. Flashbacks have overtaken my mind. I can see a little girl, me, sitting in a dark room, terror-stricken. Eyes open, eyes shut, tears. Does anyone see me here? Being a victim or witness to countless amounts of abuse has finally taken its toll. I can't suppress it any longer. I can't deny it anymore. I don't want to be here with things being the way they are. My body is supposed to be a living sacrifice, holy and acceptable unto You, but my body houses so much pain, bruised and beaten, the store house for weary souls. I can still recall my body count. Sex. The love language I knew for years because I felt in control then. It was a mental, emotional, and physical escape, euphoric, and I enjoyed the falsity of the world that I created in my head. God, I'm in danger. I need you to get me out of this 'self-digged' grave.

I witnessed a great deal of domestic violence by way of family members' relationships growing up, and it has left me traumatized. In and out of relationships, attracted to brokenness because I was in fact broken. Trying to be someone else's healer, fixer, when I had my own demons that needed slaying. Betrayal, abandonment, and rejection. I have made love to pain more than I have made love to love. One day I'm up. The next day I'm down. One minute I'm laughing. The next hour I'm excessively crying trying to catch my breath because I feel like I'm dying. Coming down from a panic attack. My mind won't stop racing. Anxiety rises up within me and I can't think straight expecting the worst, oh the agony. God, I'm in danger. I need you to get me out of this 'self-digged' grave.

I can't suck up unresolved trauma. I can't get over unaddressed pain. And for daggone sure, I can't move on from abuse unhealed. Two times. Two attempts. Two times I wanted to stop breathing and here I am again. Waiting. For the right time and opportunity because I can't stomach life anymore. I just want to die. I'm tired! I'm tired! I'm tired! I'm tired of giving my all in life, in ministry, in relationships, in friendships, and getting smacked in the face, my cheeks hurt. The gift that you have given to me doesn't work for me. How can I pray over other people's marriages and witness them continue living happily ever after while mine has fallen apart, he doesn't want me anymore, why doesn't he love me anymore? God why am I here still? I can pray over other people's children, their safety and well-being, but my child is being abused by his teacher daily and I didn't even see the signs? I failed him. I couldn't protect my baby! God, I'm in danger. I need you

Notes

Notes

to get me out of this 'self-digged' grave.

Loss after loss after loss. God, again? I'm met with another loss, again? Another betrayal again? I'm entertaining the spirit of death again? Past and present trauma colliding. Ah. Lies, deceit, manipulation, harassment, and heartbreak. I'm bleeding out. I can't stop drinking to cope with all of this pain. That night, in my twenties, when I woke up on the floor of a jail cell, it should have been my wake up call to stop drinking, but it wasn't. Now, here I am in my thirties still coping. Nicotine, too. It calms me when I can't get a hold of myself and I want the taste to be removed from my lips, but God. I feel as though I'm suffocating and slowly dying. I'm tired of masking the hurt? Suppressing the pain? Putting band aids of strength and accomplishments on infected and untreated wounds. Be strong they say, pull yourself together they say, but when do I ever get permission to fall apart? I'm tired! I don't want to be here anymore! God, I'm in danger. I need you to get me out of this 'self-digged' grave.

When did it become not okay to not be okay? Why do I always have to be strong? Why do others see my tears as a sign of weakness? I didn't sign up to be superwoman, I never auditioned for that part. God, I know there's a calling on my life. I see the gift that You have curated within me, and I see the lives being changed, but mine. God, or it could be that my divorce has triggered all of the

Notes

pain that has been buried in the crevices of my heart and now they're coming to surface. I feel like I want to vomit. My hands are sweaty and numb. Stress spots have developed in my hair. I see the shedding. My chest hurts, but it's my heart that's bleeding out. God, my irrational and tormented thoughts are beginning to get the best of me, taking my life seems to be what's best. I just want the pain to stop. Why doesn't anyone see that I'm hurting? Does anyone care? I just want the pain to stop. I just want it all to stop. I know you said in your word that you are close to the broken-hearted, but you seem so far away! I know you said, come to me, all of you who are weary and carry heavy burdens, and I will give you rest, but when do I get to rest, when, because I'm juggling so many hats? God, I'm in danger. I need you to get me out of this 'self-digged' grave.

I want to grab the wheel, run into a river, and go away. You left the 99 for that one, but God, am I still that one? Are you going to rescue me from me? They say, hurt people, hurt people, well hurt me is hurting me. God! I am fighting for my boys, but I didn't choose this mental illness. I didn't choose the abuse as a child. I didn't wake up and say, yes, I want to think this way. I want to die today. But years of unaddressed trauma and pain. Years! God, I'm trying. I don't want to leave my boys! I don't want to leave my boys! I don't want to leave my boys! My sweet boys! I'm

Notes

tired of them seeing their mommy in so much pain wondering why she is always crying. God, I don't want to die here! God, please! God, please don't leave me in this space. It's dark here. It's lonely here. It's debilitating here. God, I'm no longer holding on, but hanging on. I feel empty. No one sees me. No one hears me. I feel forgotten. God, I'm trying. I'm fighting. Just get me out of here again, and I will do the work. God, if you do it again, I know I will have trials and tribulations ahead of me, but the spirit of suicide won't be one of them. I won't go back. I will get the help that I need this time and continue to do what you have called me to do. Trauma and pain has overwhelmed me, but God, I want to heal, I want to live, I want to be the best version of myself for my babies, but this grave won't let me go. God, do it again because I'm in danger!

Do you ever feel like you're in danger? Your mind is telling you that you're not safe not even around those who love you the most? Let's pause, breathe, and analyze what you're currently grieving and what emotions have arisen because you too may believe you're in danger, but really you're hurting.

GRIEVING EXERCISE

What are you currently grieving? What has transpired in your life unexpectedly? How are you coping with grief? Go deeper into your own pain to understand and identify the root (not the reactions) you're experiencing to the pain. Go deeper into your childhood, adolescence, up until adulthood to reflect on how you've grieved during the most excruciating and gut-wrenching moments in your life. Do you self-destruct when you are grieving by intentionally causing harm to yourself because you can't manage your pain?

Notes

Dr. Michael Quist, a sociology professor for study.com, identifies self-destructive behavior as generally being caused by loss, pain, or other trauma, often occurring early in a person's life. Self-destructive behavior appears in many forms, including antisocial, addictive and compulsive behavior, self-injury, neediness, and irresponsibility and tends to become worse if indulged. Let's take a moment to pause and reflect on your life by completing the exercise below. You will have to analyze your coping strategy by identifying your self-destructive

Notes

behaviors. I will give you an example of how you should complete the sentence.

EXAMPLE

Alcohol and nicotine were the ways I coped with the spirit of rejection, abandonment, and betrayal. I did not want to face my truth directly, therefore, I drank it away until it was suppressed deep within. I would smoke it away until the memory was no longer at the forefront of my mind.

NOW, IT'S YOUR TURN.

___________ is the way I cope with the spirit of___________. I do not want to face my truth directly, therefore I___________ away until it is suppressed deep within. I will ___________ it away until the memory is no longer at the forefront of my mind.

The way you respond to pain shows whether you're healing or not. I knew I was not healing by how I responded to pain. I didn't respond as a healed person. My response was that of a broken, lost, and deeply wounded person. It triggered the sixteen-year-old girl who was still wrestling with unhealed trauma and unresolved pain because I maneuvered through life with wounds that I bandaged with strength and achievements. But, at some point, carrying years of trauma and pain becomes exhausting,

Notes

debilitating, and can be the cause of mental illnesses. Have you tried to understand your pain? Why do flashbacks come and go? Why are you still wrestling in the middle of the night with a traumatic event that happened when you were a child? Why can't you seem to put the bottle or pills down? Why are you easily triggered and agitated? According to the National Center for Biotechnology Information, the initial reactions to trauma can include exhaustion, confusion, sadness, anxiety, agitation, numbness, dissociation, confusion, physical arousal, and blunted affect. Most responses are normal in that they affect most survivors and are socially acceptable, psychologically effective, and self-limited. Indicators of more severe responses include continuous distress without periods of relative calm or rest, severe dissociation symptoms, and intense intrusive recollections that continue despite a return to safety. Delayed responses to trauma can include persistent fatigue, sleep disorders, nightmares, fear of recurrence, anxiety focused on flashbacks, depression, and avoidance of emotions, sensations, or activities that are associated with the trauma.

I beat myself up for years for how I responded to and carried pain while believing that it was a reflection of my faith. I didn't understand why I was extremely sad most of

Notes

the time, had nightmares, and frequent flashbacks. I ran to alcohol to bottle up the pain and I couldn't comprehend why. Again, I believed it was only me who responded this way, not knowing I had a mental illness. Elijah shows us that mental illness is not a reflection of our faith because our allegiance to God does not make us immune to trauma and pain. We are human and God understands how at times trauma can give us a distorted view of reality and depending upon its severity clinical help may be needed to recover.

At times it is hard to get out of the bed, shower, wash your face, and brush your hair as you grieve. The tasks that were once simple begin crippling you. In order to enter into the journey of healing, grieving is important. In her book *A Time to Grieve,* Bertha G. Simos writes, "People are prevented from experiencing the feelings that should necessarily follow loss in order to ensure a healthy resolution of the trauma. Increasingly, unresolved grief is being recognized as the forerunner for a wide range of physical, mental, and emotional disorders." All that you are presently feeling or have experienced in the past is a part of grieving. Whether you were shamed or criticized for your feelings, I hope you will understand that all you have experienced or bore witness to, was a lot for you to endure, and it has impacted you greatly. But as Simos noted, you have to feel the pain. This is self-work, and it might be one of the hardest things you have to do in order to feel, relive, and work through in preparation for your healing. But understand this, you have the best coach and teammate, God and Elijah cheering, guiding, and leading you along the way.

It is also important to pray and assess who has access to you in this season of your life. I call it the "Healing Circle," and we will dive deeper into this concept in the latter part of the book. Still, be cognizant of the spaces you enter. Simos also stated, "Because our society emphasizes competence, adequacy, strength, and accomplishment, the bereaved are often prevented by family and friends from expressing their true feelings." For this reason, again, everyone cannot have access to you in this season and it does not make them less of a friend or of importance in your life, but your wounds are open, and are at the mercy of panic attacks, heightened anxiety, and deepened depression. Protect your space. You will have to unlearn and undo a lot of what you have been taught about grieving in order to heal. Meditate on Psalm 126:5, "Those who plant in tears will harvest with shouts of joy." There are many other scriptures that talk about crying because it is healthy and should be normalized amongst

Notes

Notes

the wounded. Tears are an external release of pain stored internally.

For this reason, your environment and the spaces you enter will either have a positive or negative impact during this time. Who you allow to have access to you during your season of grief, and as you move into healing, will have an impact on how you mourn, internalize, and externalize your pain. You have to become mentally and emotionally present to your pain, and yes, it does hurt, but aren't you tired of carrying that hurt? Don't you want to release all the weight you've been carrying? Psalm 55:22 says, "Give your burdens to the LORD, and he will take care of you. He will not permit the godly to slip and fall." He won't let you fall! In order to heal, you have to give yourself space to grieve. In order to heal what you've been suppressing, you must allow it all to come to the surface, and face it, knowing that this time you aren't doing it your way, but God's way. Give yourself permission to feel everything you're going through. You cannot skip over the grieving process prematurely and progress to the post-healing phase when you're still bruised and wounded because the root of your issues will still be unaddressed. Not giving yourself space to grieve, mourn, and heal after enduring traumatic experiences and losses is unhealthy and can lead to unhealthy coping mechanisms.

Notes

It is okay to fall apart at the seams right now and feel the pain of what has caused your heart to break. One of the things I did not do for a long time is give myself permission to grieve, which triggered suicidal ideation. I tried to get over it rationalizing that everyone deals with pain and trauma. I had to give myself permission to grieve the loss of my marriage, my son being abused, the unaddressed childhood trauma, and everything in between. You must give yourself a moment to feel it too.

Whether it's to cry, scream, or question God, He can handle it. He knows you have questions because He has answers. God wants you to come to Him with all that you feel, your brokenness, pain, weariness, and questions because your current situation did not catch Him by surprise. Bishop T.D. Jakes once said, "Our feelings are a conglomerate of our experiences. They are built off of our history, not our destiny. They are your response to what happened, not what's about to happen." There is a happy ending on the other side of your pain. Romans 8:18 says, "Yet what we suffer now is nothing compared to the glory he will reveal to us later." God has a record of turning the impossible possible, transforming victims to victors, and defeat into triumph. Your grieving process is the response to the pain you've endured, but giving space to feel it is healthy.

Notes

Grieving is not where you are staying; it's only a season you are going through, which means dealing with your issues will produce healing that will manifest itself into wellness and wholeness. Healing is on the horizon and it's yours. Don't rush the process, instead sit at the feet of God and feel everything that's coming to the surface because you can't heal what you fail to confront. Breathe.

A TIME FOR SELF-DISCOVERY

BREATHING EXERCISE

Take three deep breaths. You are inhaling and exhaling. Inhaling your experiences, sitting with them, and then exhaling, releasing it over to God.

THE FEELING WHEEL

IDENTIFYING TRIGGERS

I feel triggered because: ______________________________

______________________________.

It causes me to feel these three emotions:

________________, ________________,

________________. It makes me remember: ___________

____

________________.

RECOVERY PLAN

I plan on taking care of myself by: ________________

______________________________,

______________________________________,

DECLARATIONS

I am: ______________________________,

______________________________________,

____

HEALING SCRIPTURES

Space to write scriptures, i.e.

____

____

____

____

____

____

____

____

____

____

CHAPTER THREE

A Time to Heal

"He heals the brokenhearted and bandages their wounds."
Psalm 147:3

Chapter song: God Wants To Heal You by Earnest Pugh

When one thinks about healing, and what they have to go through, they may think something is wrong with them and wonder: am I broken or in need of being fixed? If you are looking at yourself as "damaged goods," then Psychologist , Dr. Nicole LePera has a gentle reminder for you while on this journey of self-preservation, healing, and wholeness. She captioned an Instagram post, "You were never broken. Just coping. Just surviving in the ways you were shown to. We are all born whole, worthy, and complete. Healing is just discovering this truth." This was such a powerful statement and as I was scrolling through Instagram one night it spoke to my spirit. I had to keep this as a gentle reminder for myself when I have those days when I am feeling overwhelmed and beating myself up for taking steps forward just to take a few steps backwards. I had to realize that healing is not a straight race to the healing line. No, there are detours and wrong turns along the way. For this reason, be gentle with yourself and know you are not alone. God has seen your tears. He has heard your prayers. He has seen you wrestle with the troubles and trauma from your past and present, and His hand will always be on you. God desires you to be healed, whole, and well. What you've been carrying is too heavy for you to continue to carry by yourself. You're thriving publicly, but struggling and fighting battles privately. You've tried to run to others for help, but they haven't been able to attend to your internal needs. You've tried to cope by way of alcohol and drugs, and once you come down from the high and sober up, the pain is still present. You have tried to pray the pain away without addressing it. Or you may have tried to consciously or subconsciously push those painful thoughts away, locking them in a room far in the rear end of your mind, but as of late, memories have begun resurfacing.

Notes

Notes

Many times, repressed memories resurface later on in your life because you've been triggered or reminded by the traumatic event. You may be asking yourself, why after all these years am I now pondering on the molestation I never spoke of, the accident I survived, or the natural disaster that I didn't lose my life in? Perhaps, you witnessed a great deal of physical abuse growing up and no one knew you were watching? It's because you have not healed and healing hurts. There is no way around the hurt no matter what anyone tells you. Trying to escape your healing by altering your mood with alcohol, drugs, cutting, or the method that gives you a temporary release from your pain only prolongs your healing. By creating a sense of detachment, you don't address the problem head on. Psychologist, Dr. Thema Bryant-Davis stated, "Disconnecting from yourself can keep you from feeling the pain, but it can also keep you from healing."

Healing requires feeling and you can't afford to continue sucking it up. You can't heal by repression or suppression. You can't heal by failing to acknowledge what has caused your pain. You can't heal by simply getting over it. You can't! God can't heal what you won't allow Him access to. You will have to dig into your innermost parts that are so painful it causes your voice to shake if spoken aloud. God wants the best for you and the best version of you but you walk around functioning in dysfunction because you have a high tolerance for emotional pain. The unaddressed pain is slowly having an effect on your decision making, emotions, and reactions, because you're still hurting. You need to release it, confront it, and heal completely, and as a result, it's going to sting. Yes, it's painful, but there's beauty for your ashes, and joy, peace, and happiness on the other side of this.

To better understand what is meant by repression and suppression. Good Therapy, a website that helps people find the right mental health professionals, defines repression as a thought, memory, or feeling which is painful for an individual, which causes the person to unconsciously push the information out of consciousness and become unaware of its existence. The repressed thought may still affect behavior, but the person who repressed the thought is completely unaware of its existence or effect. Repression can sometimes be mistaken for suppression. Unlike repression, suppression is when a person consciously forces unwanted thoughts, memories, or feelings out of conscious awareness. Take a moment and ask yourself, why have I repressed or suppressed my thoughts for a long period of time?

Notes

Notes

I too, suppressed my pain, but once it came to surface, as bad as it hurt, I arrived at a place where I wanted to heal, and this is the journal entry written during this time. It reads...

JOURNAL ENTRY - JANUARY 2020

Here it is, here I am. A few short days after that night. The night I attempted my last suicide attempt. God, I'm going to live. I'm going to live to see your promises be manifested in my life. I'm going to live to see complete healing and wholeness. I'm going to live and fight through the thoughts that hold my mind captive. I'm going to live until I'm on the other side of this. I'm going to live by pausing so I can regain my strength. I'm going to live by removing my mask and detaching myself from the voices and opinions of others in how I should be healing in order for you to heal my wounds, spoken and unspoken.

I'm going to live because I haven't touched the surface of what you are going to do through me. I'm going to live so I can hear your voice again because I haven't been sensitive to it lately. I'm going to live and sit so I can be poured into because I have been serving and pouring into others' cups while mine is filled with air. I'm going to live by choosing me in this season, it's not self-ish, it's self-less. Honestly, I've been operating out of a painful place for a very long time and I can no longer operate in this capacity. I'm going to live because my purpose is bigger than the crushing that I've been enduring. I'm taking it all off, stripping down, taking a rest, so I can heal, so I can live. I'm going to live because my babies need me. They need their mommy. I know healing is not easy nor does it feel good, but I am believing that I will be on the other side of this better, stronger, and wiser than before! This is my season of weeping, self-preservation, and healing so I can be spiritually, mentally, and emotionally well.

Prior to my last suicide attempt, which was a few days after Christmas of 2019, I was in therapy for two months, but healing really began after the suicide attempt. Being on the brink of death reminded me I didn't want to die. I just wanted the pain to stop and to stop bleeding. I was exhausted and my life became unmanageable. All I saw was red and I believed the thoughts that terrified me because I lacked control over myself. I knew prayer alone was not the answer to my problem and God showed me this because I understood that my thinking was abnormal and irrational. Habitually, within the body of Christ, we're quick to tell others when they're experiencing trouble to "Pray about it" or "Take it to the Lord and

Notes

Notes

leave it there." However, God taught me that every biblical principle is not a one-size-fits-all approach. For this reason, discernment and wisdom is critical because no journey is identical even if there are similarities. Your journey is yours and their journey is theirs. Remember, this is why it's very important to stay in your own healing because what may be tolerable for someone else may be terminal for you. God could be requiring you to dig deeper and go further in your healing journey than the person next to you. Your pain and trauma may have impacted you more severely and God is not requiring you to just pray about it, but disconnect, spend more one-on-one time with Him, seek therapy, or seek medical attention for an antidepressant that will positively regulate your emotions.

God revealed to me that I need both biblical and clinical principles in my life. It was in therapy where I started to believe again and that I was needed, loved, and adored by God. I was diagnosed with post-traumatic stress disorder and major depressive disorder with anxiety and substance abuse. Despite the diagnosis, I am still loved by God, chosen, called, anointed, redeemed, and forgiven. Receiving the diagnosis helped me greatly because it gave my trauma language and now I can get the tools I need to manage and cope in a better and healthy way. While in therapy, my therapist introduced me to the story of Elijah because I felt crazy. God used my therapist to speak to my darkness and show me there's still light in darkness through Elijah's story. I wondered how I, as a woman who professes her love for Christ, could be suicidal again. I felt unworthy, but once I was introduced to God's blueprint for healing through the story of Elijah I immediately began to cry because I see how tender and compassionate God was with him. I entered into therapy badly wounded, suicidal, and feeling as though I had failed in every part of my life. I believed that God no longer loved me and I was damaged goods, but isn't it just like God to send a gentle reminder in the midst of our storm? It was confirmation to me that He's with me and that I need to heal from all I've endured in order to move forward. God strategically placed me in the care of a therapist who not only addressed my mental wounds, but my spiritual wounds as well. This is why, at times, prayer alone is not the solution dependent upon each person's journey because God equips therapists to help His children too.

It's important to understand the benefits that healing brings from an emotional, mental, physical, and spiritual standpoint, but also from a medical one; to be aware of the impact that trauma has on the brain. Trauma changes

Notes

Notes

your brain; the way you process pain and the way you respond to it. You are storing a lot of traumatic memories in your mind, and even though they may not be in the forefront of your mind, once triggered the memory will resurface.

A friend of mine called me one day, and immediately I felt the heaviness of her heart, and as she took a moment to breathe before any words came out of her mouth, I could feel the exhaustion. I could tell she'd been struggling with her thoughts and wanted to share them with me, but anxious about what I might say, she said. "Can, I'm suicidal." I didn't say a word because I knew that it was the first time she told anyone, and I knew she wanted me to hear her heart for a moment, so I listened to understand and didn't respond. Once she finished talking, she kept the conversation at surface level, not going past what was currently taking place in her life. I asked her if I could speak now because I wanted to ensure she said all she needed to. I then asked her about her childhood, and she began to cry. I repeated what I heard her heart saying and not her words. I told her I understood why the present situation has caused her pain, but I also knew it was deeper than that and the present situation triggered situations from her past. She then began to speak of her childhood trauma

Notes

and soon realized that the situation she was presently experiencing caused her to remember childhood pain and unaddressed trauma. The wound was bandaged without it being healed, therefore, once triggered she immediately felt the pain of her past while trying to cope and manage the pain of the present day. Those around her were dismissing and minimizing her pain and reaction to it which caused her to sink deeper into her depression, ultimately becoming suicidal. I spoke life and love into her by reminding her that her pain, emotions, and feelings were valid after all she suffered. I also gently told her that she would have to take a moment to get away from the voices of others and ask God to surround her with individuals who can discern and see beyond the surface and not just tell her to suck it up.

At times, you will have to disconnect from the voices that don't align with your spirit and you will know by the way your spirit responds—the shifting of your energy, and the heaviness you feel once the conversation is over. God-connected conversations will lighten the load you're carrying, not add weight. The healing process is your time to undo and unlearn old ways of coping and to see God for yourself and to understand and abide by how He wants you to heal. You have been holding onto unheard, unseen, and unhealed pain and trauma

Notes

because no one in your circle has given you permission to not be okay. Again, as the "strong friend," you've had to suck it up, move on, get over it, but is that what God wanted for you to do? Matthew 6:33 reads, "Seek the Kingdom of God above all else, and live righteously, and he will give you everything you need."

I operated by what others thought I should be doing because I was not strong enough to stand in my truth and was also ashamed of it. It took time, but I had to realize that in order to heal, I must let go of the shame and guilt I was carrying. There is shame that comes with enduring traumatic experiences, whether it was sexual or physical abuse, bullying or physical altercations, cheating or abandonment. And, it doesn't matter whether you witnessed or experienced it. Whatever happened, if there's no release of self-blaming, then you will continue believing that you were willing to participate in the abuse that you've suffered. Take a moment, and read this slowly: there was nothing you could have done better and it was not your fault. For this reason, release the shame and guilt that you've been carrying all of these years and heal. Let's pause, reflect, and complete the exercise below.

SELF-DISCOVERY EXERCISE

What is your truth?

____

____

What scares you the most about addressing your pain directly?

____

____

What feelings and emotions arise when you think of traumatic moments?

____

____

What is one thing you wish others understood about you?

____

____

What shame are you still carrying?

____

____

What do you know about therapy? Would you attend therapy?

____

____

Everything that God allows is not sent to make you stronger, some things are allowed to bring complete healing to

Notes

you. While you're in a season of pain, it doesn't seem that way nor does it feel good, but once you make it to the other side—and you will—you'll look back and be thankful that God took you through the valley because of the person that you've become. It's a hard truth, but we need the rain. Maya Angelou once said in an interview,

> "What I know is that it's going to be better. If it's bad, it might get worse, but I know that it's going to be better. And you have to know that. There's a country song out now, which I wish I'd written, that says, 'Every storm runs out of rain.' I'd make a sign of that if I were you. Put that on your writing pad. No matter how dull and seemingly unpromising life is right now, it's going to change. It's going to be better. But you have to keep working."

Now is your time to put in the work to heal. It's your time to address the root of your pain and not just what's at the surface level. In order to heal you must identify the root of the pain, the root of your behavior, and the root of the trauma in order to understand, and it will be helpful to you. If you do not give yourself permission and time to heal, you will begin to self-destruct. I didn't give myself time to grieve for years and suppressed an enormous amount of pain, which ultimately led me to take matters into my own hands. I began to self-medicate, indulge in self-destructive behaviors, and began having suicidal ideation at the age of

Notes

sixteen. This is your time to pull away, heal, and not place self-imposed expectations on yourself.

During this journey of healing remember God's timing is perfect. Don't limit your healing to thirty days, sixty days, or ninety days, instead allow God time to do what He's doing within you. It might be accelerated or it might decelerate. We know that God is the creator of time and can perform miracles in an instant or prolong them. There are times when you'll wallow in your pain and think "why is it taking so long for me to heal?" Or you might prematurely jump ahead of God and re-enter spaces unhealed. The question is, how do you know you're healed? How much time does it take? Is healing ongoing? Remember, God's timing is perfect. In Isaiah 55:8-9, it reads, "My thoughts are nothing like your thoughts," says the Lord. "And my ways are far beyond anything you could imagine. For just as the heavens are higher than the earth, so my ways are higher than your ways and my thoughts higher than your thoughts." Again, every journey is different, and we can't place healing on a timeline. God might have you sit and rest in your healing for weeks to months, or months to years, but you will know when you are healed by the way you respond to your triggers. In an Instagram post, Therapist Nedra Glover

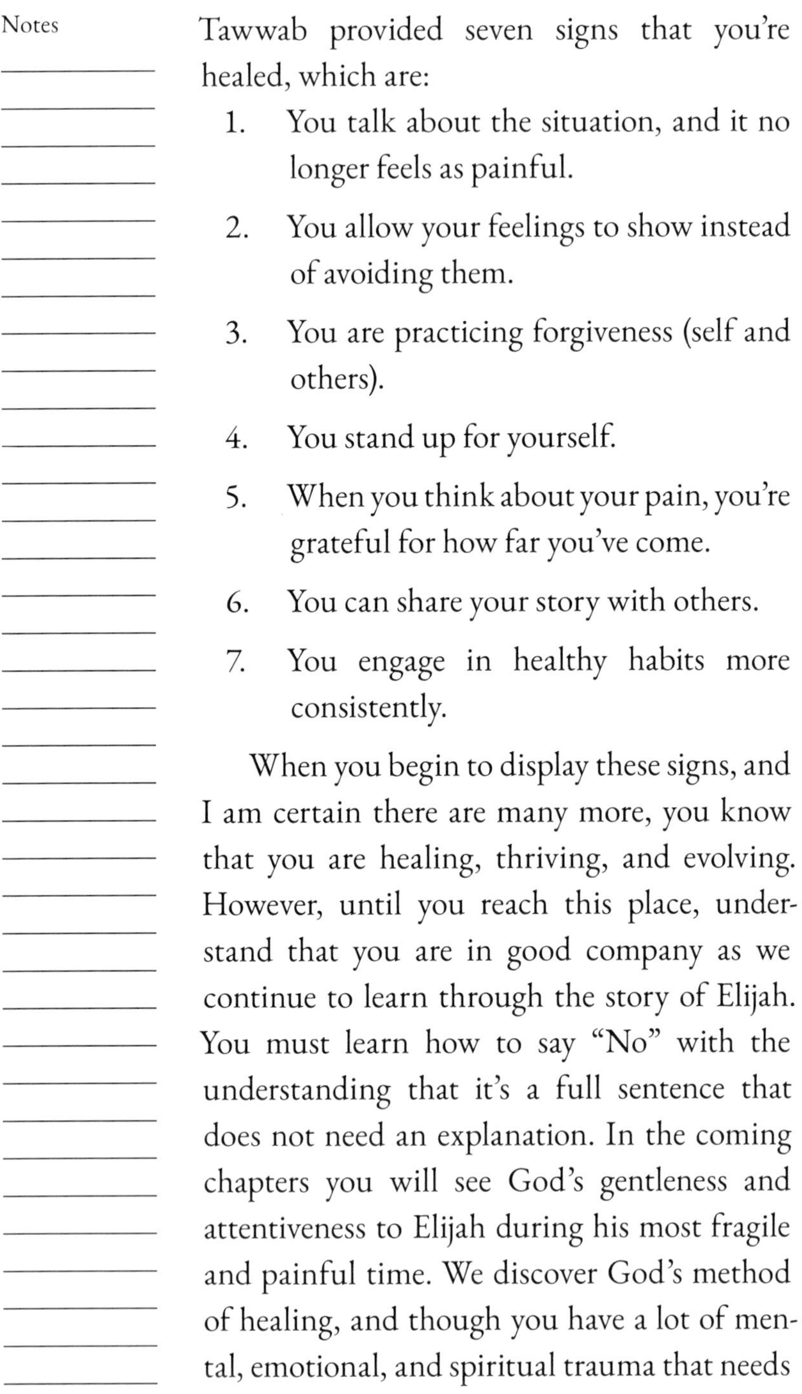

Notes

Tawwab provided seven signs that you're healed, which are:

1. You talk about the situation, and it no longer feels as painful.
2. You allow your feelings to show instead of avoiding them.
3. You are practicing forgiveness (self and others).
4. You stand up for yourself.
5. When you think about your pain, you're grateful for how far you've come.
6. You can share your story with others.
7. You engage in healthy habits more consistently.

When you begin to display these signs, and I am certain there are many more, you know that you are healing, thriving, and evolving. However, until you reach this place, understand that you are in good company as we continue to learn through the story of Elijah. You must learn how to say "No" with the understanding that it's a full sentence that does not need an explanation. In the coming chapters you will see God's gentleness and attentiveness to Elijah during his most fragile and painful time. We discover God's method of healing, and though you have a lot of mental, emotional, and spiritual trauma that needs to be addressed and attended to, you will soon discover at times God attends to our physical needs first. Now, let's examine the phases of healing that Elijah underwent amid his time of despair in part two of the book, God's blueprint for healing.

Notes

A TIME FOR SELF-DISCOVERY

BREATHING EXERCISE

Take three deep breaths. You are inhaling and exhaling. Inhaling your experiences, sitting with them, and then exhaling, releasing it over to God.

THE FEELING WHEEL

IDENTIFYING TRIGGERS

I feel triggered because: ____________________.

____

It causes me to feel these three emotions:

____,

____,

____

RECOVERY PLAN

I plan on taking care of myself by:

____,

____,

____

DECLARATIONS

I am:

____,

____,

____

HEALING SCRIPTURES

Space to write scriptures, i.e. ____________________,

____,

____

____

____

____

____

____

____

CHAPTER FOUR

A Time to Rest

"Then Jesus said, "Come to me, all of you who are weary and carry heavy burdens, and I will give you rest. Take my yoke upon you. Let me teach you, because I am humble and gentle at heart, and you will find rest for your souls. For my yoke is easy to bear, and the burden I give you is light." Matthew 11:28-30

Chapter Song: Safe In His Arms by Vickie Winans

In 1 Kings 19:1-5, we left off in our study with Elijah running away from Israel due to the death sentence that Queen Jezebel ordered after the Mount Carmel challenge where her prophets were slaughtered. Elijah was sitting under a broom tree, weary, suicidal, and in need of healing. He had lost hope, felt helpless, and believed

Notes

all of his efforts up until that point were useless. He was extremely tired and experiencing spiritual trauma. What's spiritual trauma you may ask? A part of the definition of trauma is an emotional response to a terrible event. Elijah believed the Lord would grant an unparalleled and astonishing outcome due to the Mount Carmel challenge and his obedience to the Lord. He was not expecting a wicked ending and Queen Jezebel's response. Elijah probably thought, "After all I've done, it's still not enough!" Perhaps, he forgot about Queen Jezebel or assumed she would have disappeared after the truth was revealed. In today's day and age, the phrase, "If it isn't one thing it's another," is often used. You just purchased a new car, and not even a week later you're in an accident. You just started a new job, and soon thereafter you have to take off repeatedly because your child is sick. You enter into a new relationship and immediately find out you're sharing your partner with someone else. You just receive your paycheck, and an unexpected bill is mailed to you causing you to have to reexamine your budget. This is precisely what Elijah was feeling after Queen Jezebel's death threat.

The emotional, mental, and spiritual suffering that Elijah encountered manifested itself physically. The guilt, shame, and worthlessness

Notes

became too heavy for him to bear and he lost interest in what once brought him fulfillment—ministry. In 1 Kings 19:5-9, the first thing God did in the midst of Elijah's suicidal episode was provide Elijah with uninterrupted rest and nourishment for his body. It is important to note that when you're being tormented emotionally and mentally, the thoughts that plague your mind can manifest themselves physically and cause fatigue, panic attacks, and insomnia. Read 1 Kings 19:5-9, and make note of what God does for Elijah by answering the questions below.

STUDY QUESTIONS

1. Elijah was sleeping under the broom tree when an ________ appeared telling him to get up and eat.
2. The ________ had ________ and ________ prepared for Elijah to eat.
3. Elijah was awakened________ times to nourish his body.
4. Elijah had time to rest and nourish his body giving him strength to travel for ________ days and________ nights to Mount ________.

The most important thing that stood out to me after reading verses five through nine was that God didn't ask Elijah any questions

Notes

about the state of pain he was in. Instead, God intentionally and strategically met Elijah's physical needs before addressing his mental, emotional, and spiritual ones. God looked beyond his faults, irrational thinking, hopelessness, and He saw Elijah's needs. He didn't minimize or dismiss Elijah's pain, but He gave him time to rest.

I can recall God also giving me a moment to rest. I wasn't well mentally, emotionally, spiritually, or physically. At the time, I was still serving in ministry, but not believing what I was saying or hearing. Not taking the time to properly heal caused me to become physically exhausted to the point that I began to have insomnia. At times I would take sleeping pills or drink until I became sleepy. Most nights I was afraid to sleep because I was afraid of my dreams. I would have tormenting nightmares that caused me to wake up sweating, heart beating profusely, and my mind racing. Many mornings I would wake up crying not wanting to get out of the bed. I spent two days straight in bed one time. At this moment in my life, my ex-husband was living in Germany, and the boys and I were residing in Maryland. I needed support, but at the time I didn't want anyone to know how badly I was struggling, not just with the boys, but I was declining mentally and emotionally. I couldn't even muster up enough energy to get out of the bed. I didn't shower. I barely ate, and I ignored the calls of family and friends. I wrote this journal entry during this time. It reads...

Notes

JOURNAL ENTRY- FEBRUARY 2020

Today, I got up. For the last two days, I stayed home from work. I pressed my way to handle things for my children and then I would climb back into bed. I cried most of the day away and slept the other half of the day. I listened to worship music. I tried to write out my pain and asked God does He see me? Does He hear me because the thoughts in my mind were haunting me? As I watched Braxton play on the floor, I couldn't stop crying. God, I'm exhausted. My body hurts. It goes numb sometimes. My heart aches. Is it the heartbreak or is something wrong? Headaches are becoming my norm. God, everything hurts and I am downright tired. My eyes hurt from crying excessively not to mention the massive bags underneath my eyes. Those were my thoughts, but today, I got up. I pressed my way to Bible study and said I'm not laying down anymore. I may feel a little weak in my body, but I am getting up.

Today I got up because I believed that's what I was supposed to do, get up, keep it moving, and don't stay down. Even though I was completely falling to pieces, I did the opposite of what my body and spirit was telling me to do, rest, but as I was

Notes

attempting to get dressed to continue on with my hectic and overwhelming daily schedule, I began crying again from fatigue and I heard God say to me "You need to rest. You are doing too much. It's okay to say no sometimes and rest!" Today, when I got up, I looked in the mirror, and saw the weariness in my face and realized God was actually telling me it's okay to lay back down and rest. I was actually afraid to rest because I was afraid of sleeping with my thoughts, of laying idle with my mind, and confronting what I was hesitant of, the pain and trauma, but God reminded me, "No, you're not resting in the natural, you may be sleeping in the natural, but you are resting in me. You will have peace while you rest." I stayed home and had help with my boys and that was the best rest I received in a very long time. It was uninterrupted rest, and to my surprise free of tormenting nightmares. Today, I didn't get up, but I woke up, and continued to lay down giving myself permission to rest my fatigued mind, body, and soul. I will get up tomorrow.

While studying Elijah's story I asked God, "After all the hell Elijah was experiencing you told him to rest first, why?" God answered me by leading me to Matthew 11:28-30. I don't typically read the Bible in The Message translation, but this particular day I did, and it reads,

"Are you tired? Worn out? Burned out on religion? Come to me. Get away with me and you'll recover your life. I'll show you how to take a real rest. Walk with me and work with me—watch how I do it. Learn the unforced rhythms of grace. I won't lay anything heavy or ill-fitting on you. Keep company with me and you'll learn to live freely and lightly."

My God! I have to pause again after reading this. Wow. This speaks to my heart every time. At this time in my life, I was exhausted and was simply trying to live. I didn't know how to say "No." When God led me to this text, Jesus was saying to me, your life has become unmanageable and you've been carrying your burdens on your own, and ultimately trying to figure it out on your own. Give your burdens to me, give your trauma to me, give your pain to me, and rest because only I can give you true rest. I wanted rest. I wanted to live. I wanted to recover. Therefore, I gave it all to God, and then He began disconnecting me from my comfort zones and having me tell people, "No!" The word, "No," is similar to a curse word to me because I didn't know how to say it without feeling guilty, but I did. By turning down invitations, removing myself for a moment, and being intentional about who had access to me, I began to feel lighter because now Jesus was carrying me through that season since I was no longer holding onto all of the things that caused my heart to break. Just

Notes

Notes

as God met Elijah's physical need to rest, God also met my physical needs in order for me to rest. He provided me with an in-home nanny to assist me with my children in order for me to get more rest and be able to attend therapy. He put me at a place of employment where if I needed to call out I could without any shame. Lastly, God told me to pause in ministry in order to focus on my recovery and healing. For these reasons, I was able to rest. I started noticing I was able to fall asleep quicker while I was sober. I prayed to God that He would remove the taste of alcohol and nicotine away from me in order for me to rest and heal soberly. I also noticed that when I would fall asleep, it was peaceful, uninterrupted, and prolonged rest without emotional and mental torment. I would wake up feeling refreshed and it gave me what I needed to endure and be strong enough to sit with my inner child in therapy and to confront my trauma head on because physically I was feeling better.

The Centers for Disease Control and Prevention (CDC) reports that adults need seven or more hours of sleep per night for the best health and well-being. How many hours of sleep are you receiving at this time? The CDC also reports adults who were short sleepers, receiving less than seven hours per twenty-four hour period, are more likely to report ten

Notes

chronic health conditions compared to those who got enough sleep, depression is one of the ten chronic health conditions cited. Depressive symptoms can lessen when you're able to rest. I had to realize the importance of pausing to rest. Experiencing a mental breakdown caused me to analyze what I was lacking, and rest was one of those things. After reading Bessel Van Der Kolk's *The Body Keeps the Score,* I recognized how our bodies keep a record of every traumatic event we've experienced. The analogy I frequently use is that our bodies are our temple (1 Corinthians 6:19-20), but for those who are traumatized, our bodies have become hoarders of pain. In our bodies are rooms filled with inner-child memories that we've put a bolt lock on, a living room filled with adolescent dysfunction that we learned to sit in, and basements of unseen abuse that no one knows about. Our bodies do keep score which is why many of us escape our homes and manage our pain outside of the home. You don't want to stay in the moment or in the home so to speak so you escape. In Kolk's book he mentions,

> "We experience our most devastating emotions as gut-wrenching feelings and heartbreak. As long as we register emotions primarily in our heads, we can remain pretty much in control, but feeling as if our chest is caving in or we've been punched in the gut is unbearable. We'll do anything to make these awful visceral sensations go away whether it is

Notes

> clinging desperately to another human being, rendering ourselves insensible with drugs and alcohol, or taking a knife to the skin to replace overwhelming emotions with definable sensations."

Profound! How many of us have escaped our homes and operated outside of ourselves to feel good? Remember, now it's your time to face the trauma, stop running, clean out your bodies, and release the pain in order for your body to go back to God's original intent—to be a temple where the Holy Spirit dwells, not your trauma and pain. God is no longer allowing you to escape your pain, but He is giving you the rest that you need in order to face it, soberly feel it, and heal from it. Take a moment and ask God: how does rest show up in my life at the moment? What can I say "No" to in order to have time to myself so that I can rest? Can I use my voice to speak up and ask for help to take the load off of me in certain areas where help is needed? Ask God to lead and direct you because rest is an important factor in your healing journey. God told Elijah that if he didn't take a moment to rest, then the journey ahead would be too much for him. This is your time to rest. It's okay to take a step back because if you don't give yourself permission and room to take a break eventually you'll break. Rest!

STUDY ANSWERS

1. Angel

2. Angel, Bread, Water
3. 2
4. 40, 40, Sinai/Horeb

A TIME FOR SELF-DISCOVERY

BREATHING EXERCISE

Take three deep breaths. You are inhaling and exhaling. Inhaling your experiences, sitting with them, and then exhaling, releasing it over to God.

THE FEELING WHEEL

IDENTIFYING TRIGGERS

I feel triggered because: ____________________.

____

It causes me to feel these three emotions: ____

Notes

____,

____,

____.

It makes me remember:______________________________

____

RECOVERY PLAN

I plan on taking care of myself by:

____,

____,

____.

DECLARATIONS

I am: ____,

____,

____.

HEALING SCRIPTURES

Space to write scriptures, i.e. ______________________________

____

____

____

____

____

____

CHAPTER FIVE

A Time to Reflect

"So all of us who have had that veil removed can see and reflect the glory of the Lord. And the Lord—who is the Spirit—makes us more and more like him as we are changed into his glorious image." - 2 Corinthians 3:18

Chapter Song: Let Go by PJ Morton

Following Elijah's time of rest and nourishment, which attended to his physical need, he had the energy and strength to journey on for forty days and nights to Mount Sinai (Horeb), where the Lord was waiting on him. God then attended to Elijah's mental, emotional, and spiritual needs since he was physically well. In verse nine, God asks Elijah a profound question, "What are you doing here, Elijah?" Let's pause for a moment and

Notes

ponder on this question. God, who is all knowing and all powerful, asked Elijah, "What are you doing here," as if God didn't already know the answer to His question. It's good to note that God does not ask questions without there being an astonishing reason. He asked Elijah this question twice because He wanted to give him the opportunity to express his frustrations and put language to the pain he was experiencing. This is similar to what happens during an initial therapy or intake session. Typically, before diving into anything, the therapist or intake counselor will ask the same question, "What brings you here? What in your life has brought you to the point to seek help?" Elijah at this time in the text, was having a one-on-one encounter with God. He cried out to God in verse ten about all he had done in Israel and told God, who already knew all that had taken place in Israel, that Queen Jezebel now wanted him dead. Let's spend a couple of minutes here, specifically verses ten through fourteen. I want you to read these verses then pause to allow God to speak to you. Write down what has been revealed to you after reading this passage. Particularly, pay attention to God's response to Elijah speaking on how trauma had shown up in his life because trauma has shown up in many of our lives as I wrote in my next journal entry.

JOURNAL ENTRY - MARCH 2020

Notes

Trauma has shown up for me. I never fully understood until I sought after higher education to understand how brains are wired, what causes people to think the way they do, what causes people to behave the way they do, and what causes people to mentally breakdown the way they do before understanding how trauma has shown up for me. I didn't know the language of my own pain as well as I knew the language of others' pain. Entering into therapy has given me the space and opportunity to talk about how trauma has shown up for me. Being diagnosed with Post-traumatic Stress Disorder and Major Depressive Disorder with Substance Abuse and Anxiety gave me oxygen. I haven't been breathing for a long time. I haven't been living for a long time. Just simply existing, but now, I have the language to the impact that trauma has had on my brain. Trauma has shown up for me.

No longer did I believe I was going crazy and losing my mind. I now have the language to decipher through my rational and irrational thoughts further understanding how trauma has impaired my thoughts, behavior, and feelings. I understand why I used sex, alcohol, nicotine, and avoided others, at times, trying to escape the pain because I did not effectively know how to manage the pain in a healthy way. It was my defense mechanism and avoidance strategy. Trauma has

Notes

shown up for me.

Causing me to enter into unhealthy relationships because the unhealed little girl within me just wanted to be loved and cared for even if it was painful love, unhealthy love, I got enough even if I deserved more. I learned how to be full on little. I had suicidal thoughts because I endured too many unexpected outcomes that I believed I didn't deserve. Too many heartbreaks. Too many broken promises. Too many betrayals. But due to my irrational thinking I failed to realize the part I played. Trauma has shown up for me.

I had to face my truth, which God had to reveal to me. I was attracted to brokenness because I too, was broken. Trauma is magnetic and has joined many together because they've mistaken shared trauma for compatibility because when you connect to a person you also connect to their trauma and everything that they've been through. It's a mess. Being equally yoked extends far beyond church attendance. It's a lifestyle. Being terrified to be alone after being left alone. Being mommy, daughter, sister, friend, everything to everyone while not even being present for myself. Terrified. Left alone with yourself afraid of what you might do to yourself. Going to therapy, and starting to see a change, but still scared. Talking it out. Still scared. Trauma has shown up for me.

God these are all of my crazy thoughts. You are giving me space. This is why I am here right?

Notes

To talk it out? God some days, I feel as though I am making strides, other days I do not. Maybe like today where I see the progress, but still trying to shake the past. I feel your gentleness even now. In the midst of my rambling. It has been overwhelming at times. Overpowering too. However, talking it out, I feel heard. I feel accepted. I feel seen. I feel loved. Because if I can come to you. Sit in therapy sessions. Be unfiltered, raw, and open, I see why you have shown me Elijah because trauma has showed up for him too. You understand that the failure of my marriage was not the first time I felt anger, pain, brokenness, sadness, loneliness, uncertainty, or abandonment. Trauma has shown up for me throughout my life. And talking it all out. Talking about the cycle that I want to break. The reasons behind why I am here again, self-harming, is because I never had space to feel. Trauma has shown up for me.

I had to suck it up and put a bandage of strength on it which has prevented healing and gave rise to survival. I survived my past bout with depression and suicidal thoughts, but now, I must address and heal, not just survive. Trauma has shown up for me. But so have you. God, you told me in the midst of my pain and suffering that you will cover me. I sat up one night listening to a sermon by Pastor Sarah Jakes Roberts, and you used her to say to me,

"Your purpose is on the line. I have to separate

Notes

you in order for me to finish what I started within you, but I'm going to cover you while you begin again. What was once common to you, I will have to separate you from and you're going to have to go through this season alone. You are going to have to feel a little bit lonely, but I will cover you and I will cover you when you can't connect with people the way you used to. I'm going to cover you when you risk the vulnerability that comes with surviving. I'm going to cover you when you reenter the workforce and you're not in this thing alone. Any tongue that rises up against you, I will condemn. I'm going to cover you. No weapon formed against you shall prosper. There is going to *be a hedge of protection around you when you begin again. What keeps you from beginning again is that you don't want to hurt again. Now you ask me, God, why do I have to begin again? It's because I don't want you to make your comfort zone your God! I am your God and I can only show you the power of me when you step outside of your comfort zone and dare to begin again. You're going to have to forgive, forget, begin again."*

Trauma has shown up for me. But your words have comforted me. And though trauma has shown up for me, so has grace, mercy, love, kindness, gentleness, and compassion. Your healing power is showing up for me. Things are beginning to change for me. I am starting to see clearer. Hear you clearly. Things are shifting. Trauma showed up in my life. But God, you, validated my hurt, pain, and trauma. Showing me that by speaking the hurt from my mouth is releasing it from my body where it no longer dwells. I have the power. I have the power over my thoughts. I have the power over my behavior. I have the power over my feelings. I can't control the actions of others, but I can control mine. I can't control the pain that others have caused me, but I do have control over how I respond to the pain. Trauma has shown up in my life, but so have you.

How has your trauma shown up in your life through your behavior and actions? I had to realize that alcohol and nicotine were not the problem, instead they were the methods I used to escape my pain. Therapist Nedra Glover Tawwab shared how trauma can show up in your life. She listed the common ways which are:

1. Substance abuse issues
2. Risky sexual behaviors
3. Shame
4. Dysfunctional family patterns
5. Domestic violence
6. Unhealthy relationships
7. Self-sabotage
8. Sleep issues
9. Unhealthy boundaries

Notes

Notes

10. Mental health issues
11. Codependency
12. Emotional health issues
13. Disorder eating

SELF-DESTRUCTIVE BEHAVIORS EXERCISE

There are several more ways that trauma shows up in our lives, but using the list above, take a moment and reflect. How has trauma shown up in your life? Did it make the situation better or worse for you and why? What is one behavior from the list that you have displayed but didn't put a name to? For example, I didn't realize that an unhealthy boundary of mine was accepting unacceptable behavior in relationships because I did not stand firm on my non-negotiable of creating boundaries.

I allowed what should have been a non-negotiable to be negotiable because I had abandonment issues and feared being left after giving my heart to someone. I had to realize it was deeper than what's shown at surface level for me, but had more to do with internal issues which began in my childhood. Sometimes you have to talk through your pain and give voice for your inner child to speak. Therapist Caroline Strawson once said, "The only person who can go back in time and pick up that precious child you were and make them feel safe, seen, lovable, and free from pain...is you." Pause, breathe, and reflect on the questions below.

Notes

INNER CHILD EXERCISE

What happened in your childhood that you never spoke of?

____

____

If you gave voice to your inner child what would be spoken?

____

____

What is your inner child still holding onto?

____

____

Why is it difficult for you to release it?_______

____

If you, as an adult, could speak to the wounds of your inner child what would you say?

____

____

Notes

Back to 1 Kings 19:10-14, now that you have read, aren't you amazed at how gentle God was with Elijah? Did you notice God's response? He did not rebuke, condemn, or shame Elijah for his emotional and mental state. He gives Elijah space to talk out his frustrations about the unexpected outcome following the Mount Carmel challenge. This is a prime example of the benefit of therapy as it gives space to share our experiences through the lenses of someone who is not listening to respond, but listening to understand and provide a space where safety is given and judgement is not. In verse eleven God tells Elijah, "Go out and stand before me on the mountain." During that moment, four events take place: a mighty windstorm, earthquake, fire, and then the sound of a gentle whisper. God was not present in the first three events, but God was present in the gentle whisper. Immediately, Elijah wrapped his face in his garment. Take note of God's absence and presence.

God has made extravagant gestures to His people by ceasing rain, healing a dead boy, and releasing fire from heaven at Mount Carmel, but in that moment, God knew Elijah needed a gentle presence and a soft, tender tone because of his vulnerability and fragility. Just like you and I, we respond to the voice of others differently based upon their tone. When you are hurting, you're frail and do not need an

Notes

aggressive tone of voice. When you are in pain, you are weak at times, and do not need voices that will kick you when you are already down. You need voices that will lovingly and gently give you a voice of reason and comfort to assist you in getting back up. Why do you believe tone matters when engaging with a depressed person? Has anyone been aggressive with you in their approach? How did it make you feel once the conversation was over? Do you still open up to this person? If so, why?

It's important to analyze who you allow to speak into your life, not just at this time, but at all times. Someone can possess all of the knowledge and wisdom in the world, but have poor delivery. Again, tone matters. For these reasons, God reminds Elijah again through His gentle whisper that He is still in control. This gave Elijah a moment to breathe. Having a moment to breathe calmed Elijah and reminded him that God was still with him. Again, in verse eleven, God asked Elijah the profound question, "What are you doing here?" Even though Elijah's pain was valid, his thoughts were still irrational as he continued to complain about

Notes

the unexpected outcome following the Mount Carmel challenge. This is why healing takes time. God was getting through to Elijah, but still needed to extend patience and grace in the process of getting him completely well and whole.

Elijah continued to grumble about being the only prophet left who was serving God which was not true. Obadiah was still in Israel. There were also one hundred prophets that God hid in a cave from King Ahab and Queen Jezebel. But when you are overwhelmed and blinded by pain, your view of reality can become distorted because you can't see past your own pain. God had to lovingly and gently correct Elijah's thinking by reminding him, though he felt alone, he was never alone as there were other prophets in Israel who never bowed down to Baal and Asherah. And as you continue to read 1 Kings 19, you will learn, as did Elijah, that there were seven thousand others who worshipped God. Even still, Elijah did not understand how God was working in the midst of all he'd experienced. It can be considered, given Elijah's bout with depression and suicidal ideation, that he felt worthless wondering how to move forward, also after experiencing spiritual trauma.

In the natural, trauma is defined as an emotional response to a terrible event like an accident, rape, or natural disaster. However, when it comes to spiritual trauma, it can be defined as a spiritual disaster. In Elijah's mind, he believed he had just experienced a spiritual disaster, after all the work he put in to show the Israelites who the true and living God is, after serving, after carrying out God's commands, he believed he had nothing to show for it. Just like in the natural world, trauma can paralyze us causing amnesia—it is called dissociative amnesia. The Cleveland Clinic defines it as a person blocking out certain information, often associated with a stressful or traumatic event, leaving the person unable to remember important personal information. Elijah was experiencing spiritual dissociative amnesia because the trauma impacted his psyche in such a way that he forgot how great our God is, but our God, who is so loving, continued to extend grace, compassion, and patience to him.

Elijah also harbored feelings of worthlessness. If you turn back to 1 Kings 19:4, Elijah cries out saying, "Take my life, for I am no better than my ancestors who have already died." The statement, "I am no better" conveys how Elijah saw himself. He didn't have much confidence in himself. He didn't believe he was worthy of carrying out such trusted assignments especially after his bout with depression and suicidal ideation. Elijah was

Notes

Notes

carrying deep-rooted wounds prior to arriving in Israel because if Elijah was well mentally, emotionally, and spiritually, then his first response wouldn't be suicide. He would have gone to God with Queen Jezebel's death threat, and believed that God would again perform a miracle. However, he didn't because the death threat triggered something within him. Queen Jezebel was not the cause of his mental breakdown, but the trigger to already unaddressed wounds. Elijah was so wrapped up in his pain that he was not thinking straight and wanted to escape. And even though Elijah asked God to die, he really did not want to die because if death is what he truly wanted, he would have stayed in Israel and surrendered to Queen Jezebel instead of running. He just wanted the pain to stop. Half of Us, an organization that raises awareness about the prevalence of mental health issues, when discussing suicidal behavior stated, "Most people who are suicidal don't actually want to die. They just can't see any other way to end their pain." And Elijah too, just wanted the pain to stop, which is why he decided to retreat from everyone, but death was never in God's plan for him.

When God gave Elijah time to talk that is really what Elijah needed. Though Elijah's thinking did not immediately change, God was still patient. To address Elijah's feelings of worthlessness, and to provide him with reassurance, and direction, God needed to remind Elijah that He had not changed His mind about the ministry that had been birthed through him. For these reasons, God gives Elijah an assignment, an opportunity to reset, so that he can continue on with his ministry and the call on his life.

Notes

A TIME FOR SELF-DISCOVERY

BREATHING EXERCISE

Take three deep breaths. You are inhaling and exhaling. Inhaling your experiences, sitting with them, and then exhaling, releasing it over to God.

THE FEELING WHEEL

IDENTIFYING TRIGGERS

I feel triggered because: ____________________.

____

It causes me to feel these three emotions: ____________

____,

____,

____.

It makes me remember: __________________________

____

RECOVERY PLAN

I plan on taking care of myself by: ________________,

____,

DECLARATIONS

I am: ____,

____,

____.

HEALING SCRIPTURES

Space to write scriptures, i.e. ____________________

____

____

____

____

____

____

____

____

____

CHAPTER SIX

A Time to Reset

"Let your eyes look straight ahead, And your eyelids look right before you." - Proverbs 4:25

Chapter Song: You Say by Lauren Daigle

After Elijah had time to heal, and it wasn't overnight, God gave Elijah an assignment. He met his physical, emotional, mental, and spiritual needs and then sent him back out. God didn't allow Elijah to stay in his current state, soaking, and feeling sorry for himself believing that God could no longer use someone who struggled with depression and suicidal ideation. No, God knew Elijah needed a boost in his confidence, self-esteem, and worth. For this reason, God reassured, affirmed, and strengthened Elijah reminding him that nothing

Notes

could separate him from His love nor did the lull he experienced change God's mind about the ministry He entrusted Elijah with. No one, not King Ahab or Queen Jezebel, not even Elijah's own actions, could stop the call on his life. This reminds me of 1 Peter 5:10, "In his kindness God called you to share in his eternal glory by means of Christ Jesus. So after you have suffered a little while, he will restore, support, and strengthen you, and he will place you on a firm foundation."

God gave Elijah an assignment, and this was comforting to me. It was a self-awakening moment realizing that my depression, anxiety, alcoholism, abuse, trauma, divorce, nothing, can separate me from the love of God nor change His mind about me. As such, it shows us that God is our comforter, restorer, and redeemer. And though you may have experienced depressive episodes, suicidal thoughts, and more, God still loves you and has a plan for your life. Furthermore, God has not changed His mind about you. Even after all Elijah had suffered, and his response to trauma, God still had a plan for him to continue on with his journey. God spent time with Elijah, confirming, reaffirming, strengthening, and reminding him of his greatness. The text does not say how long Elijah was in the cave, however, we do know that it was not overnight, which

Notes

lets us know to not put a time frame on our healing because God's timing is perfect. When Elijah was mentally, emotionally, physically, and spiritually well, to keep him moving forward and not focusing on the past, God gave him an assignment.

Let's take a look to discover the assignment that God gave Elijah by reading 1 Kings 19:15-21. Write down Elijah's assignment.

____

____

____

____

God was getting ready to dethrone King Ahab and Queen Jezebel. God told Elijah to go back out and anoint three men: Hazael to be the king of Aram, Jehu to be the new king of Israel, and Elisha as Elijah's own successor, who first served as Elijah's assistant in carrying out God's commands. God giving Elijah a right-hand man met Elijah's practical need of not feeling alone. He had the security of knowing there was someone next to him who was like minded. God was still meeting Elijah's needs.

When you've become acquainted with depression or any form of mental illness that gives you a high tolerance of emotional and mental pain, it can be tempting to allow it to become your comfort zone. You've been hurt more than you've been happy. You've been sad

Notes

more than you've been joyful. You've been so accustomed to crying that you've forgotten what smiling genuinely feels like. Therefore, it is natural to be fearful once you're on the other side of being hurt and sad, and you're now finding your voice, healing, and breathing. You are unlearning and learning while having a new mindset and outlook on life. You've now created a safe space with God where you now understand that you can go to Him with anything and everything. You enjoy getting to know yourself and God more, so God cannot let you stay in the cave forever. Just like He gave Elijah another assignment, you will have to re-enter spaces, create boundaries, identify safe spaces, and be cognizant about every aspect of your life, and that will be your assignment moving forward. You have to be vigilant of every friendship and activity in which you engage, because your wellness will depend on it. God has called us to live in peace and harmony, not constant pain and turmoil. Keep your eyes set on Him. Isaiah 26:3 is a gentle reminder, "You will keep in perfect peace all who trust in you, all whose thoughts are fixed on you."

Furthermore, understand before you begin to enter into spaces, you are entering differently. Your behavior has changed. Your mindset and responses have changed. You are more aware of yourself so you may not connect with everyone, because they knew the "hurt you," but now you're showing up as the "healed you." Remember, though you have the power and tools, this is an ongoing journey and healing is not linear. You are constantly learning your triggers and sore spots and will be seeking God and your therapist for resolution. In the next chapter, we will dive deeper into therapy and the tools that committing to therapy will provide to you.

Keep in mind, all that God has taught you, and keep it at the forefront of your memory. The enemy will try to feed you lies, reminding you of your past and all you've been through. He'll tell you that you're unworthy of grace, love, and restoration. Even when the enemy says these things, pull out your weapon, which is the Word of God, and give him the truth because your past does not define you. What you've recently experienced does not define you. It is God who defines us. Our experiences only shape us and are used for His glory. Your future is far better than your past. Meditate on Romans 8:18, "Yet what we suffer now is nothing compared to the glory he will reveal to us later." For this reason, let us look at the Lies, Truth, and Facts exercise.

LIES, TRUTH, AND FACTS EXERCISE

Notes

Notes

In this exercise, on the left side you will place the lies the enemy has told you about yourself that have attacked your confidence, self-worth, and self-esteem. On the right, you will place the truth that God has spoken into you such as, you're loved, you're forgiven, you're beautiful, etc. Lastly, in the middle you will support God's truth with facts—His Word, write out the scripture reference in the middle by searching through the Bible.

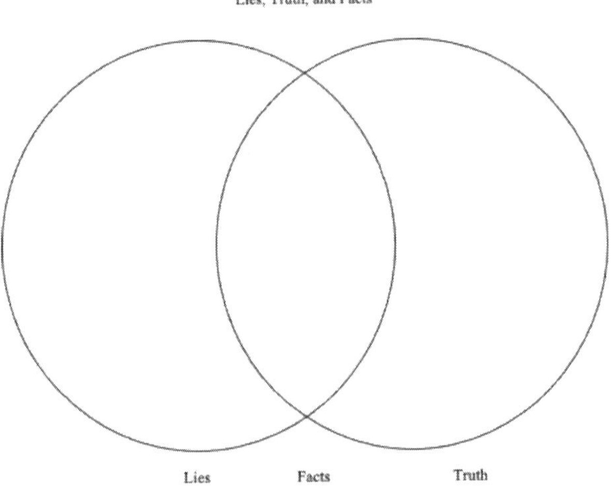

Always remember this exercise, pull it out of the book, if needed, and place it on your mirror in your bathroom or somewhere close. Re-entering spaces is not easy, there will be those who know the old version of you, and they will constantly try to remind you of your past, but you must remember who you are and

Notes

whose you are! I too, had to re-enter spaces, and in my next journal entry I share my thoughts.

JOURNAL ENTRY - APRIL 2020

Resetting. I have anxiety about re-entering into spaces. Engaging into conversations. I have been in a spiritual cocoon for some time now. How do I re-engage? What do my friendships look like now that I am beginning to open up again? I'm not the same Candace. My mentality is different. My outlook has changed. I've found new hobbies and joys. Resetting. I have nausea sometimes when I think about it. I have become accustomed to only speaking to the same seven individuals. I have become accustomed to hearing from God without feeling the need to ask other voices for their opinions.

Resetting. I have my reservations. I know that a lot has changed. Therapy has given me insight into the deep crevices of my heart and mind. I now understand why I have allowed unacceptable behavior from others. I understand why I avoid and retreat often due to the fear of being hurt or judged. I understand why I engaged in unhealthy relationships, have caused myself harm, and self-medicated often. I understand now. Resetting. Though I have anxiety, nausea, and reservations, I feel deep down inside, that I can re-enter into spaces. I can minister again. I can love again. I can trust again. I have spent a

Notes

lot of time with God. I have spent a lot of time hearing from God and being sensitive to His voice.

Resetting. It's not always easy to get back out there after you've experienced public and private battles, but I do believe Romans 8:28, "And we know that God causes everything to work together for the good of those who love God and are called according to his purpose for them." I know you will use my story for your glory. I know my mess will turn into your message of restoration, hope, and love. I know the journey ahead of me will not always be easy and without trials and tribulations, but Lord, continue to guide and teach me. Continue to speak through my therapist giving me continuous insight and knowledge on how to navigate through this world! God, I am ready! So, ready, re-set, go! This is resetting.

Moving forward and going back out into the world, after retreating and spending time in solitude with God can be uneasy for some. Life will continue to throw curve balls and at times, it'll be one after another. However, meditating on John 16:33 can help; it reads, "I have told you all this so that you may have peace in me. Here on earth you will have many trials and sorrows. But take heart, because I have overcome the world." Therefore, take heart for the one you serve has already overcome every situation that you will experience pressing ahead. You can't journey through life walking in the

Notes

sun every day because eventually the rain will come. Storms will still pass you by. However, God is telling you this will be the last time you continue through this cycle of pain and turmoil due to unaddressed trauma. You may ask yourself why you keep experiencing the same pain, same heartbreak, same failures and mishaps, same trauma responses. It's because you never took the time to heal. You only survived and survival is not conquering. If you take the time to heal, you will not have to visit this season of your life again because all of the rooms within you will be decluttered and cleaned out. It's time for you to experience true peace even in the midst of a chaotic world. Dr. Tony Evans, senior pastor of Oak Cliff Bible Fellowship, said, "Peace does not mean you will not have problems. Peace means your problems will not have you." Remember, you hold the power! Power over your thoughts, your mind, and your behavior. Therefore, you don't have to hoard trauma and pain anymore. You've had enough relationships that were only lessons, you're a scholar now. You've had enough financial hardships, you're an experienced accountant now. You've had enough lessons, now it's time to implement what God has taught you. Meditate on Joel 2:23-27:

> "Rejoice, you people of Jerusalem! Rejoice in the Lord your God! For the rain he sends

Notes

> demonstrates his faithfulness. Once more the autumn rains will come, as well as the rains of spring. The threshing floors will again be piled high with grain, and the presses will overflow with new wine and olive oil. The Lord says, "I will give you back what you lost to the swarming locusts, the hopping locusts, the stripping locusts, and the cutting locusts. It was I who sent this great destroying army against you. Once again you will have all the food you want, and you will praise the Lord your God, who does these miracles for you. Never again will my people be disgraced. Then you will know that I am among my people Israel, that I am the Lord your God, and there is no other. Never again will my people be disgraced."

At any point on this journey, you can take a moment to rest when needed to give yourself space to retreat and reflect. Lastly, after you've rested and rejuvenated yourself mentally, emotionally, physically, and spiritually, continue to grab hold of the practical tools that you will learn in part three because your time is now.

A TIME FOR SELF-DISCOVERY

BREATHING EXERCISE

Take three deep breaths. You are inhaling and exhaling. Inhaling your experiences, sitting with them, and then exhaling, releasing it over to God.

THE FEELING WHEEL

IDENTIFYING TRIGGERS

I feel triggered because: ______________________

____

It causes me to feel these three emotions:

____,

____,

____.

It makes me remember: __________________________

____

RECOVERY PLAN

I plan on taking care of myself by: ________________

____,

____,

____.

DECLARATIONS

I am: ____________________________________

____,

____,

____.

HEALING SCRIPTURES

Space to write scriptures, i.e. ________________________

CHAPTER SEVEN

A Time to Speak

"A time to tear apart and a time to sew together; A time to be silent and a time to speak." - Ecclesiastes 3:7

Chapter Song: You Are Welcome by Psalmist Raine

There has always been a stigma surrounding mental health and therapy, especially for believers. There are Christians who do not believe in therapy, believing that God is all they need. I am not one of those believers, because, dependent upon each situation, there is a level of trauma that will require more than prayer. According to John 16:33, all of us will have trials and tribulations, but when you are deeply wounded, traumatized, and grief stricken, clinical assistance is necessary. However, of late, the body of Christ is beginning

Notes

to progressively move towards embracing and speaking out about mental health. Leaders are encouraging their members to seek therapy if needed and bringing trained and professional mental health counselors into their churches to conduct seminars on holistic wellness and wholeness, particularly around mental health. Even though there are some who still believe in prayer being the only solution for emotional and mental wounds, there are a great deal of studies and research that support believers going to therapy to address their internal wounds. TalkSpace, an online and mobile application that connects people with licensed therapists when providing guidance on therapy for believers, states, "When people practice their religion seriously and believe in the healing power of God or other divine forces, it can be hard to accept the idea of a therapist providing mental enlightenment in addition to what they receive from their faith-based communities."

We have become conditioned and taught to "just pray about it. Take it to the Lord and leave it there," with no basis of application in what that looks like. This very familiar scripture in James 2:17, "faith without works is dead," is the missing piece to the application portion—the work. To drive this point home, I want to share the New Living Translation version of the text, which says, "So you see, faith by itself isn't enough. Unless it produces good deeds, it is dead and useless." Faith by itself isn't enough! Meditate on that for a moment. What in your life have you left at the feet of God believing that you didn't have to put in any work, but God told you to pick it up and do some work?

Notes

Simply put, we must do the work, and in this case, the work is therapy, and it provides us with a number of benefits. Dr. Susman, an assistant professor in the Department of Psychology at the University of Kentucky, has reported twenty benefits of therapy, but I will identify eight of the twenty benefits:

1. Have a safe and private place to talk about sensitive personal issues
2. Better understand symptoms and diagnosis
3. Become informed about additional effective treatment options
4. Decrease or eliminate depression and anxiety
5. Reduce and manage negative or destructive thoughts, feelings and behaviors
6. Understand and process effects of traumatic events

Notes

7. Reduce impulses and actions of self-harm or aggression
8. Plan for crises to ensure safety and reduce risk of harm

Being able to understand your trauma history, implement a plan of action, identify coping strategies, and further understand oneself can be both beautiful and painful. For this reason, it's important that biblical and clinical principles collide because the benefits outweigh eliminating one piece of the puzzle—you need both. Author Darren Pierre strongly believes that faith and therapy work together and should not be mutually exclusive. He stated, "For me, it is no difference than faith and medical health. Yes, prayer is a strong tool for change, but to activate that prayer and faith, attention from a medical professional is necessary." To process the painful and traumatic events in your life, therapy is work and God is where your faith rests knowing that you will get through it and become better for it.

I've always believed in therapy, but once I accepted my diagnosis with no shame and guilt, I knew I had no more time to waste in putting voice to my pain. This is the reflection phase. God gave Elijah time to reflect on the totality of his life, giving him the opportunity to talk it out by asking him "Why are you here?"

Notes

This is therapy. I sought out a Christian-based therapist and got to work. I needed my therapist to speak my language both clinically and biblically.

Therapy has also given me space to breathe. Now I understand what's going on, and I need the tools that therapy provides to combat my own thoughts. My diagnosis will no longer have power over me. When my therapist introduced Elijah's story to me, it not only provided me with a self-awakening moment, but it reminded me I'm not in this alone. God did not have me in a cave somewhere, but practically He allowed me to experience the same blueprint He had Elijah undergo. God gave me strength to do my work in therapy and it's renewing my mind and still edifying me in every session. I've had to do a lot of unlearning and rewiring my brain to not catastrophize, which is automatically anticipating the worst.

I'd become overwhelmed with anxiety which caused me to think about the worst possible outcome to all situations. It's as if my mind automatically goes dark. My therapist always says to me, "Candace, you're always anticipating things to go wrong, but what if they go right?" The more I began to go deeper in identifying the root of my anxiety and catastrophizing, the better I became in creating a plan to manage the pain and anxiety when

Notes

it comes. Therapy has also given me deep revelations and tools to use to continue to walk in my healing, power, and authority over my thoughts, behavior, and feelings.

The Cognitive Model

Situation → **Thought** → **Emotion** → **Behavior**

something happens | the situation is interpreted | a feeling occurs as a result of the thought | an action in response to the emotion

My therapy sessions are based on the Cognitive Behavioral Therapy (CBT) approach. According to the American Psychological Association, CBT is a form of psychological treatment that has been demonstrated to be effective for a range of problems including depression, anxiety disorders, alcohol and drug use problems, marital problems, eating disorders and severe mental illness. CBT is used to change thinking patterns to assist in:

1. Learning to recognize one's distortions in thinking that are creating problems, and then to reevaluate them in light of reality
2. Gaining a better understanding of the behavior and motivation of others

3. Using problem-solving skills to cope with difficult situations
4. Learning to develop a greater sense of confidence in one's own abilities

CBT is also used to change behavioral patterns to assist in:

1. Facing one's fears instead of avoiding them
2. Using role play to prepare for potentially problematic interactions with others
3. Learning to calm one's mind and relax one's body

Over time, learning the skills and applying them to difficult situations will become customary. It will be a part of your everyday response because now you're no longer reacting from a painful place. Now you know what works for you and what does not so you can respond from a peaceful place. I didn't realize that I didn't have the tools and skills I needed because I was conditioned and taught that faith alone was enough for me until I began having depressive episodes one after another. I began fighting thoughts of suicide again. I had to realize that what I was believing to be spiritual warfare was in fact, more mental than anything for me. Take a look at my next journal entry, as I began using the therapeutic tools

Notes

Notes

learned in therapy to combat my thoughts.

JOURNAL ENTRY - MAY 2020

I attended a New Year's revival service one night and the pastor made this profound statement, "One who endures an immersed amount of trauma for years will turn to the world who caused the trauma at times before turning to God. That's why an unregulated mind is a dangerous mind." I knew I was in trouble, but I didn't know how to vocalize it. I desperately wanted God to heal all of my brokenness. I wanted to have peace and to live with no more suicidal ideation! I wanted to be healed completely, not to only survive it, but to have no residue, no shame, no guilt, and no bondage. The moment I knew that I needed help for myself without anyone's input was when I couldn't recognize myself and disconnected from those who love me. I asked God to take the taste of alcohol and nicotine away from me completely because it was a vice that I ran to when pain hit and I no longer wanted it to be my crutch. I laid it down. I laid my pen down. I opened my Bible, but all the pages were unreadable because they were soaked with tears. I thought I conquered depression. I vowed to never allow myself to go in that dark room again. I have two babies now, how did I get back in this dark room? How am I questioning life, again? He whispered to me "You shall live and not die! That grave doesn't belong to you! Erase your name off of that tombstone, it's not assigned to you! Now, come out!"

After all I've preached, spoke, wrote about! How? Why is hell's voice louder than yours? God had to meet me in that dark room and bring me out because I made my bed there. I was going deeper and deeper into depression and my thoughts were getting sicker. I couldn't sleep. My mind races constantly. Sometimes it was hard for me to catch my breath. I felt physically weak often. I just wasn't well. What I learned is you can't compare journeys as we all have our own journey to walk, and I learned that everyone doesn't heal the same! Instead of asking others how did you overcome this, I had to cancel the noise from others by stop asking and accepting their advice and ask God, how do I overcome this? Candace? In my way of thinking, in my way of feeling, in my way of processing and coping pain, how do I recover from this! It's not the problem at hand that's the issue, it's not the divorce, it's not what happened throughout my life, it's not my first son's father abandoning him, but it's the trauma connected to it that needs attention and healing.

I had to separate myself and I did so for a year! It was my season of self-preservation and I am thankful for it now! I am thankful for God putting me in therapy and with a therapist who not only understands the clinical side, but most importantly, the biblical side as well. I said God

Notes

Notes

it's me and you this time. God responded with, it's about time! And the first thing I received was you will have trials and tribulations to come, but this won't end in death and this will be the last time you will go up against the spirit of depression and suicide. In therapy, I wrestled with my thoughts and how I viewed Christianity. I wondered why the Bible speaks about depression and suicide more than the church does today. It made disconnecting easy, at times, because I got tired of the insensitive comments. I got tired of being quoted scriptures that I already knew. I got tired of this too shall pass because truth be told I believe all of it, but my mind wasn't on the same page of what my spirit knows. The fight of my life.

Think of every physical illness that you've had to overcome in your lifetime, all attacking you at once. It's tiring! Well every mental and emotional trauma that I have experienced, the failure of my marriage triggered it all for me. It uprooted it a lot. It uprooted the spirit of abandonment, rejection, neglect, depression, suicide, guilt, shame, mother-shame, postpartum, it all hit me at once and it came to take me out. I was almost out of here! I had to retreat so that I could breathe, rest, and learn how to rally in the valley. Nobody could pull me out of my dark place, but God! How could you show up to work suicidal? It's a learned behavior I learned how to show up to places broken and still produce. I had to unlearn what I learned that produced poor decisions and my response to the tragedies of life. Once I learned that I have no control over the pain that others have caused, broken promises, or the actions of others but I do have control over my response and how I cope. It was a painful place to be in, but I was convinced and believed that if I have to endure a little more pain by being committed to healing to come out of my mind then that's what I have to do!

My spiritual mothers said, "Candace, this is mental. Yes, it's spiritual, but it's also mental. People can speak life into you all they want, but if you don't believe it, things won't change." She further said, "God wants to hear your voice! Not your pastor, not mine, He wants to hear from you! This is between you and Him because only you and Him know all that you've been through! You have to take a moment, to pause, because what you believe you're going to die in is where you're going to receive healing."

Once I realized that I can heal because God is with me, I took the focus off of the trigger, the divorce, and put my focus on the root of my pain and myself to heal, recover, and become well. I had to learn that people can endure the same level of trauma, but are impacted by it differently. I learned that what is tolerable for one person may be terminal for the next. This is why you should not compare trauma and pain because no one

Notes

Notes

knows what's planted in the root. I had to analyze my friends and those around me. I paid attention to those who were there for me through my best moments in life and stuck around during the worst moments of my life. I had to separate myself from those who did not understand the season that I was in. I had to separate myself and be okay with people not understanding. I had to be okay.

Ecclesiastes 3:7 mentions there is a time to be silent and a time to speak. You have to be cognizant of the people around you because not everyone is happy about your growth. There are people who pray for you and there are people who prey on you. Being able to identify friends from foes is very critical. Oftentimes, we seek the approval of man before we make a move. We ask our family and friends what they think about this. Sometimes, we get the response or support we desire, but other times, due to the lack of support, we shut down and don't move. God doesn't want you to be associated with everyone. Remember your wellness depends on every move you make and every interaction you engage in because everyone and everything is not for you. You will have to seek God and pray about those around you to identify your healing circle, and who should be closely and intimately connected to you because your spirit will respond. When you're around the right people they will not disturb your peace with their presence.

A man in the Bible named Job, who suffered severely by the work of Satan, with God's permission, lost his children, wealth, and health. When his friends came to visit him, they could immediately see how much pain Job was in, but instead of engaging in conversation all they did was sit with Job. They did not speak or give him their opinions, in the moment, instead they sat with him in silence because at times grief is so heavy that there are no words to adequately soothe the bereaved. Job's friends understood his healing language. They knew, in the moment, it was not the time for them to speak to Job because honestly it was probably nothing they could have said to make Job feel better. He just needed their presence around him as he grieved. Having people around you who know when to speak and when to be silent is important. You need people who will speak to your healing through encouragement rather than those who speak to your pain encouraging you to engage in self-destructiveness further bringing you down to wallow in a depressive state. Psychologist Dr. Thema Bryant-Davis said, "When someone is going through a storm, your silent presence is more powerful than a million, empty words." This is why knowing your circle is important.

Notes

Notes

You will have to learn how to cancel the noise coming from others while you are in this season of healing especially if you haven't already. Entering into therapy will cause you to go deeper within yourself. For these reasons, know thyself and thy circle. If the people around you are not speaking life back to you, be quiet. I allowed certain family and friends into my pain because I thought it would soothe me, but in return I was given negative opinions and words that ate at my spirit and caused me to decline emotionally and mentally. Therefore, identifying your healing circle is crucial. Your circle should not be big, but small. My circle included seven people, which included my therapist. These were the individuals I would call on if I was having a meltdown, panic attack, or needed encouragement. Let me point out something: if your close friends or family members are not in your healing circle, it does not mean the love shared is lessened or is a reflection of your relationship. It only means in this season of your life, you have to be intentional about who you're allowing access to you because your healing circle should speak your language, emotionally, mentally, and spiritually. In the same manner as Elijah, at the beginning of 1 Kings 19, God strategically and intentionally assigned angels to feed and nourish Elijah's weary body prior to spending

Notes

one-on-one time with God in the cave. God will do the same for you because He knows who you need in this season. He will assign angels to your life to assist you in this season of your life and you will know who these individuals are because they will speak to your spirit in such a way that your spirit will connect with theirs. Bob Beaudine, the author of *2 Chairs: The Secret That Changes Everything*, discussed in his book how to identify the people who are assigned to you. He wrote,

> "How will you know? Listen to what they say. Listen to how they say it. Great friends speak on a frequency that you will be dialed in to. It's the language of love. In the midst of your toughest moment, your friend will help remind you that you have a hope and a future. This friend will help you carve away those areas in your life that are holding you back."

HEALING CIRCLE EXERCISE

When you read Beaudine's excerpt on friends who came to mind? Reflect on the moments in your life thus far, both the good and the bad. To analyze your healing circle, it is important to make note of who was present while you were on the mountaintop, but absent while you were wrestling and tarrying in the valley. It doesn't mean you love them less, but I have learned that every friend is not for every situation. Therefore, knowing your friends is important to your growth and healing. Take a

Notes

moment and complete the exercise below.

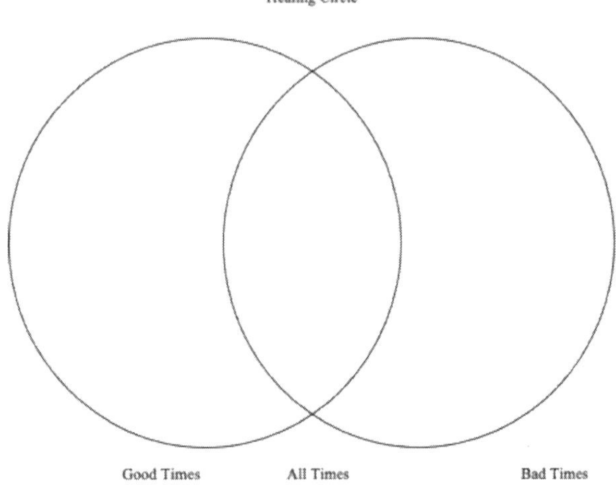

I hope in your healing circle, you didn't leave out someone who has also been there for every moment in your life, you! In this season, yes, God will send help, trusted help, but you also have to show up for yourself.

In Matthew 6:33, it reads "Seek the Kingdom of God above all else, and live righteously, and he will give you everything you need." But in reality, at times, God isn't who we go to first. We tend to pick up the phone and call on a trusted friend. There are moments when the advice redirects us back to God, and other times, can stray us further away from Him. Show up for yourself by showing up in the presence of God, first. For this reason, seeking God first is very critical while healing. Identifying your healing circle is

Notes

very critical as well because God will guide and lead you to the person you need to speak with about your circumstance, if needed, and when needed. And one of the many attributes that I love about God is He knows who we need, what we need, and when we need it. When you seek God first, He will eliminate all the confusion, discontentment, and eerie feelings and thoughts that are running through your mind by giving you the peace and the guidance that you're in need of. When facing your trauma and pain head on, be mindful of your circle, and the shifting of your energy around certain people because your wellness depends on it. You are entering into a self-construction phase where you have to create boundaries for yourself. You are beginning to love and fully embrace the healed you. Now, you must fully show up for yourself as you have always shown up for others. All of the lessons you've learned and the experiences you have lived through have shaped you in becoming the person that you've fought hard to become. Now is the time for you to embrace the new you.

A TIME FOR SELF-DISCOVERY

BREATHING EXERCISE

Take three deep breaths. You are inhaling and exhaling. Inhaling your experiences, sitting with them, and then exhaling, releasing it over to God.

THE FEELING WHEEL

IDENTIFYING TRIGGERS

I feel triggered because:

____

____

____

It causes me to feel these three emotions:

______________________________,

______________________________,

______________________________.

It makes me remember: ______________________

____

____

RECOVERY PLAN

I plan on taking care of myself by: ____________________

____,

____,

____.

DECLARATIONS

I am: ______________________________________,

____,

____.

HEALING SCRIPTURES

Space to write scriptures, i.e. ____________________

____

____

____

____

____

____

____

____

____

____

____

____

____

____

CHAPTER EIGHT

A Time to Embrace

"This means that anyone who belongs to Christ has become a new person. The old life is gone; a new life has begun!" - 2 Corinthians 5:17

Chapter Song: Deliver Me By Donald Lawrence Ft. Le'Andria Johnson

Embracing the new you requires learning the new you. This involves learning what brings you joy and what makes you smile uncontrollably to the point that your stomach is hurting from laughing so hard. For most, self-care is new because you've been accustomed to taking care of everyone else that you've neglected yourself. Raphailia Michael, a licensed counseling psychologist, defined self-care as any activity that we do deliberately in order to take care of our mental, emotional, and physical health. Taking care of yourself can include, but is not limited to the following:

1. Taking a walk through the park
2. Going for a long drive
3. Calling a trusted friend
4. Making an appointment at the barber shop/hair salon
5. Going to the movies
6. Reading a book
7. Writing in your journal
8. Grabbing your favorite blanket and lying down while listening to music
9. Taking a nap
10. Exercising

Maya Angelou once wrote, "Every person needs to take one day away. A day in which one consciously separates the past from the future. Jobs, family, employers, and friends can exist one day without any one of us, and if our egos permit us to confess, they could exist eternally in our absence. Each person deserves a day away in which problems are confronted, no solutions searched for. Each of us needs to withdraw from the cares which will not withdraw from us." We all need a moment to

Notes

Notes

unplug and unwind. We need a moment to recharge ourselves in order to be at our best in every entity that is outside of ourselves.

SELF-CARE EXERCISE

From the list above, how can you take better care of yourself? List three activities that you can commit to implementing into your schedule on a weekly basis.

Self-care is a priority for me because there was a time when I did not take care of myself. I was busy taking care of everyone else, putting myself last, and by the time I got around to myself I was too tired to do anything. I now make it a weekly, and as time permits, a daily task to take care of myself. My therapist introduced me to soaking music as another self-care technique. I'd never heard of soaking music, but was open to the idea of it. After it was explained to me, I went home and researched it further. First let me define the root word soak; it means to become saturated by or as if by immersion. I would also like to share John Belt's, the founder of Overflow Global Ministries, interpretation of soaking music. "The goal of this genre of music is to help us

Notes

rest in Jesus. It helps people find the place of rest that Christ has provided to us. It allows us time to lay down and rest with soothing anointed music. The music inspired by God's Spirit helps us to enter into His rest, let go of things and just receive in His presence."

In my opinion, soaking music is instrumental worship music. It's soothing, and more instrumental and less lyrical. However, there is soaking music that does consist of lyrics. These lyrics are short and repetitive, further causing you to sit still in God's presence and soak. Sometimes I fall asleep, so not only does it soothe me, but it gives me rest. I listen to soaking music frequently when I am overwhelmed emotionally and mentally. There have been mornings, before my feet hit the floor, that I still could feel the wetness underneath my eyes from the tears I cried the night before. This is when I would grab my phone and turn on soaking music. I welcome God into my pain and into each day by soaking. I will play music by Psalmist Raine. One song I like in particular is "You Are Welcome." The lyrics are: "I may be broken, but you are welcome. I may need your healing and I say you're welcome. I know you're able in spite how I feel, and I am depending on your world reveal."

I listen to it on repeat, allowing the lyrics to penetrate my mind, body, and soul until my

Notes

mood changes, my thoughts become clearer, and I feel at peace. There are many forms of self-care but intentionally choosing what brings you peace and joy is the important key to caring for yourself.

Another activity that has been beneficial to me is coloring. Sounds pretty juvenile, but it is therapeutic for me because my mind narrows in on the art and I'm focused in the moment detaching myself from what's going on around me. It also releases stress. I color alone, or sometimes, I make it a family activity giving my sons a page to color and we sit in the living room discussing what's in the picture and how it makes us feel. I found positive and faith-based books that have a plethora of soothing quotes and messages that fuel my mind with love, warmth, and joy. Coloring makes me smile, and I enjoy it. I take my books with me to work, carving out time to sit color, pray, and soak. I also have one lying around my bedroom to fill my time and heart when my mind would randomly wander.

Outside of coloring, I sat down one day on my deck and wrote down in my journal the activities that bring me peace, joy, and simply just put a smile on my face. I began having date night with myself at least once a week, but I made myself a promise to not go more than two weeks without having one. It became beneficial to my mental health and gave me positive and healthy ways of release. My date night would normally go like this: arrive at the massage parlor for a sixty or ninety minute massage, find Yelp's best-reviewed sushi restaurants and try a different one each date night, or go to a store to browse or shop. I love it! I switch it up of course, mixing in movies, nail salons, or hair appointments. Bottom line is, I take care of myself outside of being available to everyone else. I have learned how to give myself the love and attention I have always craved from others. I learned how to prioritize and how to balance family, friends, and myself without placing myself at the bottom of the list, and it feels good!

Embracing the new you also requires creating and strictly implementing boundaries for all you're connected to, including family and friends. You will have to learn how and when to say "No!" To be real, for most this is a foreign word because you don't know how to say it, but believe me, you better start. Let your "Yes" mean "Yes" and your "No" mean "No!" You do not have to justify your response with reasons. "No" is a complete sentence, therefore, learn how to speak up for yourself by standing in your truth. Find your voice in the moment of discomfort and let your truth be heard. No longer will you allow others to walk over you.

Notes

Notes

It's your time now and the healed you needs to be seen, heard, and loved—not silenced. If something or someone shifts your energy making you uncomfortable or you don't agree with something, speak up in the present moment. Do not let the moment pass you by where you end up taking it home with you, pondering on the event, and weeks later you're still thinking about it. No, stand up and speak up. Psychologist Dr. Thema Bryant-Davis states:

> "We begin to silence ourselves, we begin to live through a filter, this diluted watered down version of who we are. And the more I come home to me, the more I show up in the fullness of who I am, that I don't have to constantly test the waters for other people's approval, validation, opinion of me, that I get to that liberated place where I recognize the sound of my own voice, that it doesn't have to be other people's voices and opinions being projected on me and through me."

No longer are you living through a filter, hiding yourself, your feelings, and thoughts. No, the healed you, speaks, and creates boundaries for others to respect you. Again, boundaries are not just for strangers, but for those closest to you as well. Therapist Nedra Glover Tawwab, stated in an Instagram post, "You may need boundaries with the following: your parents, your kids, your partner, your time, associates, in-laws, family, friends, neighbors, exes, strangers, work, social media, and yourself!" Wow! Pretty much, you need to take

Notes

care of yourself and know when to be accessible and inaccessible. You even have to create boundaries for yourself. For example, if you throw yourself into work because it's a passion for you and included at the top of your priority list, you will have to create boundaries that reflect your time. After 6:00 p.m., it is family time, and I have to disengage from work in order to spend time with my family. That's an example of boundaries.

You have to be intentional about your time and space. You have to be cognizant of how others speak to you and treat you. You can't control the actions and behavior of others, but you do have control over the spaces you enter and conversations you choose to engage in. This applies to family as well; if you're not having a good day, you can choose to say, today is not a good day. I need to take today, to rest, reflect, and reset, maybe tomorrow. Don't be pressured into doing activities when your mental health is on the line.

Lastly, create emotional and mental boundaries. You have experienced a great deal of suffering and pain. When you reflect on these moments, be kind to yourself. Create a boundary of grace for yourself because therapy brings up old wounds and at times it's easier to forgive others for the pain that they have caused while beating yourself up. Now

Notes

is the time to embrace all that you've endured and forgive yourself because you know better now, but you didn't then. Maya Angelou said, "Forgive yourself for not knowing what you didn't know before you learned it." You've learned a great deal in this season and will continue to do so, therefore, forgive yourself. Furthermore, God has already forgiven you and will make your mistakes right. Romans 8:28 states, "And we know that God causes everything to work together for the good of those who love God and are called according to his purpose for them." Yes, everything will work out for your good! Isn't that good news? There's more good news, in this next season of your life; you will not bounce back from all that you've endured because you do not want to bounce back to the place you once were; no, now you are bouncing forward into becoming all that God has created you to be. Embrace the lessons and embrace your new season. Take a moment to read my thoughts on embracing the new me who is healing in my next journal entry.

JOURNAL ENTRY - JUNE 2020

I'm not bouncing back. I'm bouncing forward. I'm embracing the version of me that's healing. I'm giving myself permission to speak. To say what makes me laugh, sad, and cry. I'm not bouncing back. I'm bouncing forward. After all I've been through, and I'm still here! I'm still alive! I still have the love of my boys surrounding me daily! I'm thankful! I'm not bouncing back. I'm bouncing forward. I don't want to return to the same ole' place, no, it's time to move forward to new opportunities, new doors, new blessings, and new connections! I'm embracing the fullness and beauty that encompasses me. I'm learning to stand in my yes, and stand in my no. I'm learning how to create boundaries and not always being available for everyone ensuring my cup is filled. I'm not bouncing back. I'm bouncing forward. This is my season for a divine payback! Restoration is about to hit my home! I can feel it. It's happening for me. This is healing. This is freedom. This is self-love! God, I know you heard every prayer and caught every tear that I shed! It's my time now. I can finally breathe. I can breathe. I'm not bouncing back. I'm bouncing forward because the new bounce back is called bounce forward!

Embrace the season you're in and the amazing person you are becoming. Embrace the pain you've endured by inhaling it, which you are doing in your private time with God and by way of therapy, and exhale it by fully embracing all that you are. Embrace that you are fearfully and wonderfully made and that you are empowered to unlock those dark rooms in your body that housed trauma and

Notes

Notes

pain. The power that you've always had to take dominion over your thoughts, feelings, and behavior is now able to stand up fully. Don't bounce back, but bounce forward because you are no longer operating from the passenger seat. Your inner child isn't driving anymore, the version of you that's healing is now in the driver's seat. Therefore, the people who once knew you in your brokenness have to let go of who they thought you were—that version of you has passed on. You are healing, well, and whole. Depression, trauma, and pain no longer have your mind chained because they're loose. You have power over your mind because you have been reminded of God's love through the story of Elijah knowing that depression, extreme sadness, anxiety, nothing is new to God. You almost didn't make it, but you did and now it's time to reintroduce yourself. No one and nothing can stop what God is doing in your life, not even you. It's time to inhale all that you've been through and exhale all that you are now and embrace it. Embrace you because now you're no longer simply existing, now you're breathing.

A TIME FOR SELF-DISCOVERY

BREATHING EXERCISE

Take three deep breaths. You are inhaling and exhaling. Inhaling your experiences, sitting with them, and then exhaling, releasing it over to God.

THE FEELING WHEEL

IDENTIFYING TRIGGERS

I feel triggered because:

____

____

____

It causes me to feel these three emotions:

____,

____,

____.

It makes me remember: ________________________

____

RECOVERY PLAN

I plan on taking care of myself by: ____________________

____,

____,

____.

DECLARATIONS

I am: ____________________________________,

____,

____.

HEALING SCRIPTURES

Space to write scriptures, i.e. ____________________

____

____

____

____

____

____

____

____

____

____

____

____

____

CHAPTER NINE

A Time to Breathe

"I am leaving you with a gift—peace of mind and heart. And the peace I give is a gift the world cannot give. So don't be troubled or afraid." - John 14:27

Chapter Song: Be Blessed by Yolanda Adams

Have you been breathing? You've taken one whirlwind of a journey with me. We're at the end of this journey together, and I am glad you decided to come alongside me. My prayer and hope for you is that you completely heal from every hurt, disappointment, betrayal, abandonment, loneliness, and brokenness that your heart has experienced. Additionally, I pray that you heal so you believe there are people in the world who love you and want to see you healthy in every aspect while

Notes

living your best life. For these reasons, I hope you understand that you're deserving of all of the attention, love, and care that you've been searching for, needing, and giving to others.

I pray that God will place individuals around you who won't speak to your emotions and pain, nor minimize or dismiss the trauma that you're trying to heal from, but speak to your spirit and healing. We all have love languages in the spirit realm and I pray that God will place those around you who see you and hear your pain loudly, even in your silence. Don't be ashamed because what you're experiencing doesn't make God love you less because nothing can separate you from Him. God loves you and you're needed here. The grave isn't your resting place yet. God desires complete healing and for you to live in peace. It's not time for you to rest in peace yet—live! The Bible that we teach and preach from speaks on depression and suicide more than the church does today. I've heard people stand from pulpits and tell people they're going to hell due to mental illnesses, but that is not theologically sound and it's ignorant. People don't take their lives, the illness does; just as illnesses like cancer destroy the physical body. An unregulated mind is a cancerous mind so you must continue taking care of your mind, body, and soul. As you continue on your journey of healing, surrendering to God while dying to your flesh, and engaging in safe spaces, remember to give yourself permission to rest, reflect, and reset. As I have mentioned throughout the book, God has given us the greatest blueprint for healing in taking back the power over our mind which is resting, reflecting, and resetting when needed. I pray that this book has given you additional resources and tools to help you heal. My hope is that it has also encouraged you to seek out a therapist, if you do not have one already, who speaks your language of healing. Therapy will assist you in analyzing who has access to you in this season by creating your healing circle, creating boundaries, and continuing in the process of identifying your triggers and sore spots. You have to stay at God's feet and in His Word. Post your healing scriptures throughout your home or keep them in an accessible place so you can say them aloud because life and death is in the power of our tongue. Therefore, continue to take your power back by speaking over your mind and life every day. I discussed there being days where you'll feel the pain immensely and at times won't be able to speak. On these days, remember to turn on soaking music of your choice and allow your mind to soak in God's presence because tears are prayers too because they're a language that only God can understand.

Notes

Notes

Early on I told you that healing is messy and is not a straight path to the finish line. I'm sure you've taken many steps forward and other days you may feel as though you've taken steps backwards. That's okay. Don't beat yourself up on these days—cry if you have to; scream if you have to—instead, do what's necessary for you to regroup and regain control over your mind in a healthy manner. Pain hits all of us differently as you have learned. This is your healing and no one else's. Therefore, give yourself some grace. You are healing from present and past trauma, and everything that lies between the two, including pain spoken and unspoken, and trauma addressed and unaddressed. The stories shared and exercises completed in this book may have struck a few nerves and it's been brutally painful at times, but during those times I hope you felt God's presence sitting with you as He comforts, strengthens, and empowers you.

Resting, reflecting, and resetting is not a one-time process where you complete a step and you're healed. That may be the process if the pain is at the surface level. But for those who have pain planted deep in the ground, you will have to continue to repeat the steps as necessary. Even with that, a transformation has already begun in your mind, heart, and spirit. Be proud of the ground you've covered thus far.

God is calling you to rest, reflect, and reset in this season because you're exhausted and have been running on empty for far too long. You have tried to heal on your terms, your way, and He wants you to come to Him. Remember, Matthew 11:28-30, "Then Jesus said, "Come to me, all of you who are weary and carry heavy burdens, and I will give you rest. Take my yoke upon you. Let me teach you, because I am humble and gentle at heart, and you will find rest for your souls. For my yoke is easy to bear, and the burden I give you is light." God offers rest for your weary soul, your tormented mind, and your broken heart. Continue to allow God to enter into the dark crevices of your mind to show you there is always light. This is your time to transform and evolve. You will know when the true transformation of healing has begun by the response you give to your triggers because you won't respond out of pain, but healing.

For some of you, having this book in your hands has been life changing because you've been walking through life beating yourself up, and thinking you've failed, just as I did. For others of you, your faith in God has weakened because you believed that your mental illness has disqualified you from having access to Him. I hope you understand that you've been in good company because Elijah has been

Notes

Notes

where you currently are. You have digested a great deal of instruction and counsel, completed the self-discovery exercises and study questions, and have made a commitment to your healing. This alone speaks volumes about who you are. I am anticipating and ready for what you will produce in the natural because of the healing that's taking place in the spiritual realm. Remember, don't focus on the individuals from your past because you do not have to convince them of your transformation. The anointing on your life will speak for itself. Finally, let me pray over the journey ahead of you.

Father, I thank you for the opportunity you have bestowed upon me to impart into your child's life. I don't take it lightly or for granted because I understand how valuable they are to you. I thank you for their life and for their journey. Lord, you've seen the tears they've cried that no one's seen and the trauma and pain that has been buried away. I pray that you have met their needs throughout their reading and will continue to do so. I pray that now they understand how valuable, how dope, and how amazing they are to you. Let them know how much you love them and how nothing they've endured has caught you by surprise. You already knew where they would be at this moment of their life. God, as you waited for Elijah, asking him, "Why are you here?" you

Notes

didn't ask because you didn't already know the answer, but you asked because you are our answer and you care for us so deeply that you give us room to inhale and exhale our troubling pain. They can now tell Satan that the joke is on him because their funeral has been cancelled in the name of Jesus. Throughout this journey, they've made a conscious decision to not only heal, but to live life to the fullest. God, extend strength, grace, wisdom, discernment, and gentleness to them as they continue knowing that you have never and will never leave them nor forsake them. They may be at the end of this book, but they're about to begin a new journey because now they have a new way of thinking. 2 Corinthians 5:17 says "This means that anyone who belongs to Christ has become a new person. The old life is gone; a new life has begun!"

God, you came into their broken places privately, but I believe you will do a new thing for them publicly by blessing them in front of the very ones who tried to break them down. God, send Godly people into their lives who will assist in their mental, emotional, and spiritual wellness, and remove the leeches. They are not in this season alone. The pain, broken promises and every trauma-stricken relationship they entered into did not catch you by surprise. Release all of the shame, guilt, and embarrassment that they feel, and free them from self-destructive

Notes

behaviors, feelings, and thoughts. I come against every demonic attack on their life in the name of Jesus. I come against every death trap that has their name on it in the name of Jesus. They shall live and not die in the name of Jesus. God, though they have committed to healing, they need you, to place a hedge of protection around them and those connected to them in the name of Jesus because of the temptation to do wrong. Peter said in Romans 7:21, "I have discovered this principle of life—that when I want to do what is right, I inevitably do what is wrong." Spirit of the living God have your way in their life. Show yourself strong and mighty in their life and we will forever give you all of the praise, honor, and glory, in Jesus' name. Amen.

Now, breathe. Don't look back. Keep moving forward, and rest, reflect, and reset as many times as you need to because remember, healing is not linear. It's your time now!

> "My child, pay attention to what I say. Listen carefully to my words. Don't lose sight of them. Let them penetrate deep into your heart, for they bring life to those who find them, and healing to their whole body. Guard your heart above all else, for it determines the course of your life. Avoid all perverse talk; stay away from corrupt speech. Look straight ahead, and fix your eyes on what lies before you. Mark out a straight path for your feet; stay on the safe path. Don't get sidetracked; keep your feet from following evil." - Proverbs 4:20-27

Resources

ADAPT Mobile Crisis Team , 1-866-260-8000

Behavioral Health Authority , 1-877-653-6363

National Suicide Prevention Hotline, 1-800-273-8255

Suicide Prevention Emergency Number, 988

Hotlines, 1-800-Suicide, 1-800-273-Talk

SAMHSA's National Helpline, 1-800-662-HELP (4357)

SAMHSA Abuse Counselor, 1-800-774-6796

“Give all your worries and cares to God, for he cares about you.”- 1 Peter 5:7 NLT

“The Lord himself will fight for you. Just stay calm.” - Exodus 14:14 NLT

“And we know that God causes everything to work together for the good of those who love God and are called according to his purpose for them.” - Romans 8:28 NLT

“Cry out for insight, and ask for understanding.” - Proverbs 2:3 NLT

“And I will ask the Father, and he will give you another Advocate, who will never leave you.” - John 14:16 NLT

“Don’t worry about anything; instead, pray about everything. Tell God what you need, and thank him for all he has done. Then you will experience God’s peace, which exceeds anything we can understand. His peace will guard your hearts and minds as you live in Christ Jesus.”

- Philippians 4:6-7 NLT

"So letting your sinful nature control your mind leads to death. But letting the Spirit control your mind leads to life and peace." - Romans 8:6 NLT

"Be strong and very courageous. Be careful to obey all the instructions Moses gave you. Do not deviate from them, turning either to the right or to the left. Then you will be successful in everything you do." - Joshua 1:7 NLT

"For God has not given us a spirit of fear and timidity, but of power, love, and self-discipline." -2 Timothy 1:7 NLT

"For his anger lasts only a moment, but his favor lasts a lifetime! Weeping may last through the night, but joy comes with the morning." - Psalm 30:5 NLT

"I will not die; instead, I will live to tell what the Lord has done." - Psalm 118:17 NLT

"The Lord says, "I will give you back what you lost to the swarming locusts, the hopping locusts, the stripping locusts, and the cutting locusts. It was I who sent this great destroying army against you." - Joel 2:25 NLT

"And the Holy Spirit helps us in our weakness. For example, we don't know what God wants us to pray for. But the Holy Spirit prays for us with groanings that cannot be expressed in words." - Romans 8:26 NLT

"God is not a man, so he does not lie. He is not human, so he does not change his mind. Has he ever spoken and failed to act? Has he ever promised and not carried it through?" - Numbers 23:19 NLT

"My sheep listen to my voice; I know them, and they follow

me. I give them eternal life, and they will never perish. No one can snatch them away from me," - John 10:27-28 NLT

"Don't copy the behavior and customs of this world, but let God transform you into a new person by changing the way you think. Then you will learn to know God's will for you, which is good and pleasing and perfect." - Romans 12:2 NLT

"Yes, this anguish was good for me, for you have rescued me from death and forgiven all my sins." - Isaiah 38:17 NLT

"O Lord, I have come to you for protection; don't let me be disgraced. Save me, for you do what is right. Turn your ear to listen to me; rescue me quickly. Be my rock of protection, a fortress where I will be safe. You are my rock and my fortress. For the honor of your name, lead me out of this danger. Pull me from the trap my enemies set for me, for I find protection in you alone. I entrust my spirit into your hand. Rescue me, Lord, for you are a faithful God." - Psalm 31:1-5 NLT

"For I know the plans I have for you," says the Lord. "They are plans for good and not for disaster, to give you a future and a hope." - Jeremiah 29:11 NLT

"Then Jesus said, "Come to me, all of you who are weary and carry heavy burdens, and I will give you rest. Take my yoke upon you. Let me teach you, because I am humble and gentle at heart, and you will find rest for your souls. For my yoke is easy to bear, and the burden I give you is light." - Matthew 11:28-30 NLT

"He will wipe every tear from their eyes, and there will be no more death or sorrow or crying or pain. All these things are gone forever." - Revelation 21:4 NLT

"We are pressed on every side by troubles, but we are not crushed. We are perplexed, but not driven to despair. We are hunted down, but never abandoned by God. We get knocked down, but we are not destroyed. Through suffering, our bodies continue to share in the death of Jesus so that the life of Jesus may also be seen in our bodies." - 2 Corinthians 4:8-10 NLT

"God is our refuge and strength, always ready to help in times of trouble. So we will not fear when earthquakes come and the mountains crumble into the sea." - Psalm 46:1-2 NLT

"So shall they fear The name of the LORD from the west, And His glory from the rising of the sun; When the enemy comes in like a flood, The Spirit of the LORD will lift up a standard against him." - Isaiah 59:19 NKJV

"He heals the brokenhearted and bandages their wounds." - Psalm 147:3 NLT

"The Lord is close to the brokenhearted; he rescues those whose spirits are crushed." - Psalm 34:18 NLT

"I am leaving you with a gift—peace of mind and heart. And the peace I give is a gift the world cannot give. So don't be troubled or afraid." - John 14:27 NLT

"But forget all that—it is nothing compared to what I am going to do." - Isaiah 43:18 NLT

"Don't be afraid, for I am with you. Don't be discouraged,

for I am your God. I will strengthen you and help you. I will hold you up with my victorious right hand." - Isaiah 41:10 NLT

"You will live in joy and peace. The mountains and hills will burst into song, and the trees of the field will clap their hands!" - Isaiah 55:12 NLT

"Give your burdens to the Lord, and he will take care of you. He will not permit the godly to slip and fall." - Psalm 55:22 NLT

"Yet what we suffer now is nothing compared to the glory he will reveal to us later." - Romans 8:18 NLT

"All of this is for your benefit. And as God's grace reaches more and more people, there will be great thanksgiving, and God will receive more and more glory. That is why we never give up. Though our bodies are dying, our spirits are being renewed every day. For our present troubles are small and won't last very long. Yet they produce for us a glory that vastly outweighs them and will last forever! so we don't look at the troubles we can see now; rather, we fix our gaze on things that cannot be seen. For the things we see now will soon be gone, but the things we cannot see will last forever." - 2 Corinthians 4:15-18 NLT

"Even when I walk through the darkest valley, I will not be afraid, for you are close beside me.
Your rod and your staff protect and comfort me." - Psalm 23:4 NLT

"For he will rescue you from every trap and protect you from deadly disease. He will cover you with his feathers.

He will shelter you with his wings. His faithful promises are your armor and protection. Do not be afraid of the terrors of the night, nor the arrow that flies in the day. Do not dread the disease that stalks in darkness, nor the disaster that strikes at midday. Though a thousand fall at your side, though ten thousand are dying around you, these evils will not touch you." - Psalm 91:3-7 NLT

"So don't worry about tomorrow, for tomorrow will bring its own worries. Today's trouble is enough for today." - Matthew 6:34 NLT

"The Lord himself will fight for you. Just stay calm." - Exodus 14:14 NLT

"I have told you all this so that you may have peace in me. Here on earth you will have many trials and sorrows. But take heart, because I have overcome the world." - John 16:33 NLT

"The Lord opens the eyes of the blind. The Lord lifts up those who are weighed down. The Lord loves the godly." - Psalm 146:8 NLT

"'Everyone who hurt you will be hurt; your enemies will end up as slaves. Your plunderers will be plundered; your looters will become loot. As for you, I'll come with healing, curing the incurable, because they all gave up on you and dismissed you as hopeless—that good-for-nothing Zion. Again, God's Message: I'll turn things around for Jacob. I'll compassionately come in and rebuild homes. The town will be rebuilt on its old foundations; the mansions will be splendid again. Thanksgivings will pour out of the windows; laughter will spill through the doors.

Things will get better and better. Depression days are over. They'll thrive, they'll flourish. The days of contempt will be over. They'll look forward to having children again, to being a community in which I take pride. I'll punish anyone who hurts them, and their prince will come from their own ranks. One of their own people shall be their leader. Their ruler will come from their own ranks. I'll grant him free and easy access to me. Would anyone dare to do that on his own, to enter my presence uninvited?' God's Decree. And that's it: You'll be my very own people; I'll be your very own God. Look out! God's hurricane is let loose, his hurricane blast, Spinning the heads of the wicked like dust devils! God's raging anger won't let up until he's made a clean sweep completing the job he began. When the job's done you'll see it's been well done." - Jeremiah 30:16-24 MSG

"When you go through deep waters, I will be with you. When you go through rivers of difficulty, you will not drown. When you walk through the fire of oppression, you will not be burned up; the flames will not consume you." - Isaiah 43:2 NLT

References

Self-Destructive Behavior: Signs, Causes & Effects." Study.com. May 30, 2017. https://study.com/academy/lesson/self-destructive-behavior-signs-causes-effects.html.

The Centers for Disease Control and Prevention. https://www.cdc.gov/sleep/index.html

Logos Bible Software

"Trauma." American Psychological Association. American Psychological Association. Accessed July 5, 2020. https://www.apa.org/topics/trauma/.

Diagnostic and Statistical Manual of Mental Disorders. Fifth Edition. 2013

https://www.bridgestorecovery.com/major-depression/what-is-a-major-depressive-episode/

The Tony Evans Study Bible

The Tony Evans Bible Commentary

The Body Keeps The Score - Bessel Van Der Kolk, M.D.

A Time to Grieve: loss as a universal human experience - Bertha G. Simos

Trauma-Informed Care in Behavioral Health

Services:Understanding the Impact of Trauma https://www.ncbi.nlm.nih.gov/books/NBK207191/ Retrieved July 22,2020

Suicidal Behavior http://www.halfofus.com/condition/suicide/ Retrieved August 2, 2020

About the Author

Mother, Author, Minister, and Mental Health Advocate Candace Washington,better known as Candace Writes, was born in Selma, Alabama. At an early age, Candace developed a passion for writing, and at the age of twelve, her English teacher recognized her writing skills and asked if she would join the writer's club. Candace then started writing short stories and plays for her church and others in her community. In addition to writing, Candace also enjoys storytelling through the performing arts as she is a graduate of the Barbizon Modeling and Acting School in Towson, Maryland.

In 2010, she received her Bachelor's degree in Psychology from Bowie State University. In 2015, Candace became the founder of Candace Writes, LLC, and accepted the call on her life to preach and teach the Gospel of Jesus Christ. In 2017, Candace went back to school to further her education at the graduate level at

Howard University's School of Social Work, and on April 9, 2017, she became a licensed minister. A month later, she received her Master's Degree.

Candace has been featured on radio shows, the Word Television Network, and several podcasts discussing faith and mental health. Candace has a heart for God and His people. Her transparency has gifted her with a heart for this generation and fosters conversations about mental health, conveying that believers can have both our strong God and a strong therapist. Her favorite scripture is Jeremiah 29:11, "For I know the plans I have for you," says the Lord. "They are plans for good and not for disaster, to give you a future and a hope." She currently resides in Crofton, Maryland, with her sons, Bryson and Braxton.